15/12/5   R1-10

The Psychology of Spea

The Psychology of
Speaking in Tongues

by John P. Kildahl

HODDER AND STOUGHTON

LONDON · SYDNEY · AUCKLAND · TORONTO

Contents

Foreword

Until the late 1950's, in the modern era at least the practice of glossolalia—speaking in tongues—was confined to a few extreme, theologically conservative religious sects. The atmosphere in which it occurred· was generally ecstatic, even hysteric. Then, about fifteen years ago, glossolalia began to appear in mainline Protestant churches; its practice was found to be increasing among Episcopal, Lutheran, and Presbyterian congregations. The very respectability of those who now spoke in tongues, as well as the quiet way in which they did it, made the phenomenon difficult to dismiss as just another peculiar form of religious extremism.

The clergy and behavioral scientists undertook to examine the matter in depth. The clergy were concerned with its relation to the life of the church and the scientists with its bearing on individual and group psychology. It was in the context of greatly increased use of glossolalia by its members, and of heated theological discussion, that the American Lutheran Church asked Paul A. Qualben, M.D., psychiatrist; Lowell J. Satre, Ph.D., a professor of New Testament; and myself, a clinical psychologist, to investigate the practice of glossolalia in the church. The aim of the study was to help the church in preparing guidelines for church policy on the subject, from both a theological and a pastoral point of view.

When we had concluded the American Lutheran Church study, it was evident to Dr. Qualben and me that we had only begun to probe the many facets of the phenomenon, so we applied for and were granted funds from the Behavioral Sciences Research Branch of the National Institute of Mental Health, which enabled us to broaden the scope of our work. The report of this research, completed in 1971 and entitled *Relationships Between Glossolalia and Mental Health,* is available from the National Institute of Mental Health, Bethesda, Maryland.

But, as at the conclusion of the American Lutheran Church study, Dr. Qualben and I were still convinced of the value of further work in this area. We devised an independent research program, the results of which are presented here. I am exceedingly grateful for the work of Dr. Qualben, whose insights have richly leavened the lines of this volume. It would be a better book if he had been able to contribute directly to the writing. The opinions in this book, however, are not necessarily his, and I must bear the responsibility for any errors in conclusions or judgments.

The following six methods of information-gathering provided the basis of our study:

1. Dr. Qualben and I made two separate trips from coast to coast of the United States to observe and record firsthand information as to the way glossolalia was practiced in a variety of geographical and sociological areas. These two field surveys were made a year apart, the second functioning as a follow-up study which also contributed new material.

A sensitive situation was created by news coverage that resulted from the announcement of a NIMH-funded study of glossolalia. The confidentiality of our research involving human subjects was in jeopardy. Reporters knew the communities and even some of the individuals who were being studied. Because the grant received such wide publicity (e.g., why was the federal government giving away money to study speaking in tongues?), it was felt that in order to protect the anonymity of the persons involved, further research should be conducted involving locales not originally publicized. Consequently, the entire study was duplicated in areas of the United States which will not be identified. To repeat: the data in the NIMH study, and in this volume, are not based upon the original investigations publicized when the NIMH grant was received.

2. We distributed a detailed questionnaire to tongue-speakers by which they could indicate their own understanding of what influenced them to practice glossolalia. They were generous both of time and spirit in cooperating with this project.

3. To increase our coverage we carried on a wide correspondence with tongue-speakers and those familiar with this happening.

4. We interviewed a number of linguists and anthropologists as well, in order to bring their special knowledge to our study. We are particularly grateful to Dr. William J. Samarin for the contribution of his expertise as a linguistic scholar. We are grateful also to another distinguished linguist, Dr. Eugene A. Nida, whose consultations aided our work.

5. In our travels and in countless hours of discussion and deliberation, Dr. Lowell J. Satre provided a valuable historical and biblical perspective.

6. The bibliography included in this volume lists the published source material used to provide the background for our further research on glossolalia.

In order to obtain firsthand clinical experience with tongue-speakers, Dr. Qualben and I met with a wide variety of church groups committed to the practice of glossolalia. Dozens of tape recordings were made of men and women speaking in tongues. We also spoke with non-tongue-speaking prayer groups which otherwise were equivalent in every possible way to those who were glossolalists. The groups varied in size from five to fifty. Pastors, church officials, and laymen were questioned to ascertain their understanding of glossolalia. Psychological interviews and extensive psychological testing were undertaken.

The persons interviewed ranged in age from twenty to eighty years. They represented every socioeconomic class. Their education varied from the first eight grades to four years of postcollege training. They were affiliated with mainline Protestant churches, such as Episcopal, Lutheran, and Presbyterian.

Although there are many similarities, speaking in tongues by right-wing Protestants such as Pentecostalists and within the Roman Catholic Church was not clinically researched in this study.

This book is the result of ten years' concentrated study of the phenomenon of glossolalia. It has been exciting to investigate an area of human behavior which heretofore has received little scientific attention, and through it to contribute new material to the general understanding of man. I am grateful to the many hundreds of people who have helped us in our work. They range from a girl living in North Carolina who said, "Come and live with us for three weeks, and then you will really know how the Spirit of God moves our total beings, as well as our tongues," to a man at a party who, having just read in the *New York Times* that our study indicated that tongue-speakers and non-tongue-speakers were about equal in mental health, sidled up to me and whispered confidentially, "Those tongue-speakers— they're really all nuts aren't they?"

Our experience of scholars working in community has been rewarding. And there have been scores of concerned and informed persons who, through thoughtful exchanges in conversation, correspondence, and journal articles, have both contributed to my understanding and sought to add to their own.

The Psychology of Speaking in Tongues

1

A Description of Glossolalia—or Speaking in Tongues: *What Is It?*

Standing at her sink washing the breakfast dishes, Mrs. Rogers spoke out loud. She said, "Iana, kanna, saree saree kanai, karai akanna kanai karai yahai, oh saramai, saramoiyai iana kanna."

Mrs. Rogers was speaking in tongues—technically called glossolalia. She did not know what the words meant, but she felt a quiet contentment as she talked and sung the strange syllables. Some days she spoke only a word or two in this way before she changed to English, but that morning, she uttered the rhythmic sounds for about ten minutes and stopped only when she had finished scouring the dried scrambled eggs from the frying pan and had gone upstairs to begin making the beds.

Speaking in tongues still seemed strange to Mrs. Rogers, though she had been doing it for more than a year. She felt as if she had been given the ability to speak in a new language, without having to trouble too much about what the words actually meant. It was a pleasant, effortless thing to do and often filled her with a sense of well-being.

THE SOUND OF GLOSSOLALIA

If you had listened to Mrs. Rogers for a few minutes, and if she had told you that she had been raised in a foreign country,

1

you probably would have believed her. Speaking in tongues does not sound like gibberish. It has the rhythm and qualities of a language. Yet Mrs. Rogers did not make a deliberate or conscious effort to control the movements of her tongue. She told me that they did not involve thought at all. But she was not in a trance. Her senses continued to operate during the experience, because she did get the frying pan clean, and she did at the same time look out her kitchen window and watch the birds splashing in the birdbath in her back yard. However, while she was clearly in touch with her environment, there was some lessening of conscious control.

Mrs. Rogers is an active member of an Episcopal church. Of a congregation of approximately two hundred persons about thirty speak in tongues. Each one utters a different pattern of sounds, which gives the impression of being familiar only to the speaker.

HOW THE EXPERIENCE IS INITIATED

The following episode taken from our records illustrates how the ability to speak in tongues typically begins. After an ordinary evening church service, interested members of the congregation were invited to remain in church in order to discuss the gift of tongues. About a dozen of the sixty who were there stayed on. They gathered together around the altar rail, and seven of them prayed out loud in English. One of them, Bill Jones, remembered praying: "Lord, fill me with your Spirit. Use me to do your will. Open my life to your leading." Then the guest preacher for the first time during the evening, began to pray in tongues. Bill later reported, "I felt, as I listened to him praying in tongues, as if there were an electrifying charge in the air." When the leader asked if the group would like to receive the gift of speaking in tongues, several answered, "Oh yes, Lord. Oh, yes!"

They knelt at the altar as a group, and the leader encouraged them to try to "receive" this ability. He went from one to another, laying his hands on each person's head. Bill told me that with a prayer in tongues and with encouragement, the leader asked him to make an effort to move his lips in a free and relaxed manner. "Say after me what I say, and then go on speaking in the tongue that the Lord will give you." "Aish nay gum nay tayo . . ." prayed the leader and waited for Bill to repeat the same sounds, and then to go on in his own words. Bill tried. "Aish nay gum nay tayo . . ." and then stopped. "Aish nay gum nay tayo . . . Aish nay gum nay tayo . . ." The leader, keeping both of his hands on Bill's head again prayed that Bill would open himself to receive the "gift of the Spirit."

"Aish nay gum nay tayo . . . aish nay gum . . . aish nay . . . anna gayna . . . ayna ganna keena . . . kayna geena anna naymanna naymanna . . ." Bill had begun to speak in tongues. The utterances were faltering at first, with hesitations after almost every word, and they were so quiet that his wife next to him at the altar rail could not understand what he was saying. He simply uttered the strange sounds as they came to him without knowing how they came.

The leader, still with his hands on Bill's head, prayed, 'Thank you, Lord, thank you." Bill's momentum picked up, and as his fluency increased he experienced the strange sensation of uttering syllables and words and phrases that he had never heard before and certainly did not understand. He spoke for two or three minutes, then put his head down on the altar rail and cried silent, joyous tears. He later said, "It was the best I ever felt in all my thirty-one years."

Two other persons began to speak in tongues during that service. One woman said about fifteen words. Another spoke continuously for at least ten minutes. The other participants tried earnestly, and the leader exhorted them, placing his hands on their heads, but the words never came.

However, three nights later a fourth member of that group began to speak in tongues as he was getting ready for bed. A bachelor, he had been trying to be prayerful and speak in tongues as he walked about his apartment turning out the lights and closing the windows. As he sat on his bed pulling off his left sock and musing out loud, he said without thinking, "Raha, hasha mayim, maiya, meeya ehla elohim. Yaima haiya yaisu elohim." He knew at last that he was speaking in tongues. A quiet contentment settled over him. He remembered Bill's emotional display at the evening meeting a few days before and began comparing his reaction to Bill's. He knew that they did not have the same kind of personality. Bill was excitable, whereas he generally reacted calmly when new things happened to him, whether it was changing his job or beginning to speak in tongues. He felt good about this new blessing, but he wasn't one to announce it to everyone. It was typical that he should watch while others spoke and then try it out by himself in his own good time. That night he tried praying in tongues again while he was relaxing in bed. He found that he could go on at length, and he dropped off to sleep with a profound sense of well-being.

This experience confirmed to him what other tongue-speakers report: once possessed of this ability, a person retains it and can speak with fluency whenever he chooses. It does not matter whether he is alone or in a group of fellow glossolalists. He can speak in tongues while driving a car or swimming. He can do it silently in the midst of a party, or aloud before a large audience. The experience brings peace and joy and inner harmony. Glossolalists view it as an answer to prayer, an assurance of divine love and acceptance.

2

How Tongue-Speakers Describe What They Do

EIGHTEEN QUESTIONS ANSWERED

The most vivid descriptions of the experience of glossolalia are offered by tongue-speakers. As a basis of our study we put a series of questions to each tongue-speaker. The eighteen questions together with the answers we received appear below. Every reply contains the exact words of glossolalists, but they are composite answers, not the answer of any one person. Each answer is, however, representative of all the answers offered by the glossolalists.

Questions 1 and 2: How did you receive the gift of tongues? What was the first occasion of your speaking in tongues and who was with you at the time?

Answer: I was at home alone when I received the gift of tongues. I had been prayed for at several meetings in church, but didn't receive the gift then. About two weeks after one of those meetings, I received word that my only son was in trouble. As soon as I hung up the phone after talking with him, I opened my Bible and began to read out loud from First Corinthians. Suddenly some unknown speech took over, and I couldn't break

in on it to read again in English. A power had taken ahold of
my tongue and the words just flowed like water. What a joy it
was! There was a feeling of supercleanliness. I have never been
the same since.

Question 3: What are the factors which must be present in
order for you to speak in tongues?

Answer: There do not have to be any special conditions. I
can speak or pray in tongues any time or any place that I want
to. Of course, I use my own judgment about when it is appropriate to do it. But whenever I am open to God I can speak in
tongues.

Question 4: Is your tongue-speaking expressed in public or
private? Is there any difference in what happens when speaking
in tongues in solitude, in contrast to a group setting?

Answer: I use my gift of tongues mostly in private for my
own meditation. When I am alone, I do it at my workbench or
when I am driving in my truck. In public I only speak in tongues
when I feel especially led to do so. That isn't very often because
I feel a little embarrassed in front of other people. It sounds
the same wherever I do it.

Question 5: Is there any particular sequence of thought or
action which usually precedes speaking in tongues?

Answer: I don't think of anything in particular. It's just like
praying in our own language. I have a need to express myself
and to communicate with God and I let the words and feelings
go out toward Him.

Question 6: Are there any physical, bodily movements con-
nected with the experience of speaking in tongues?

Answer: No. I can speak in tongues in any physical state and
I do not act or feel in any unusual way. Of course I always get
a feeling of well-being when I pray in tongues and know that
this is the gift of God that has been bestowed upon me. The
only time that I felt anything in a particular physical way was
the first time that I spoke in tongues. At that time I felt a burn-
ing all through me, and chills and great beads of perspiration,

a trembling and sort of a weakness in my limbs. Still, I felt wonderful and clean. I don't get those physical sensations any more when I pray in tongues.

Question 7: Please discuss the part of laying on of hands in tongue-speaking.

Answer: The Bible says that the laying on of hands was done and people received the gift of tongues. So, we also do what was done then. When the pastor put his hands on my head, it gave me a greater sense of communication and contact with God.

Question 8: Can you do this "at will"? Is it "accidental" at times?

Answer: I can do it whenever I wish to do so. It has never seemed to come accidentally. It is more spontaneous at some times than others. It is as if sometimes I just break out into song without thinking too much about what I am singing. At other times, I more or less consciously plan that I am going to begin to pray in tongues.

Question 9: Can you shed any light on the question of how and/or why some people are able to speak in tongues and others are not?

Answer: I believe that it has to do with the person himself. There is a difference. There must be travail in prayer and in worship, with much repenting. I believe it depends on whether the person is open to God, and willing to accept what God wants for him. Some people may want this just for themselves, selfishly, and that may stop them from ever beginning to speak in tongues.

Question 10: Is your tongue-speaking in another language spoken somewhere in the world or does the speaking consist of words and sounds which are not a part of any known language?

Answer: I do not know what language I have and I don't question it. I believe it is from God and that is good enough for me. Although I am not absolutely sure, I think it is a definite language, perhaps a lost tongue or any other language such as Hebrew, Aramaic, etc. I know of cases where important mes-

sages have been expressed in scriptural Hebrew and Greek, often
by persons with no theological training, and only a grammar
school education or less.

Question 11: Please comment on the part which the interpretation of tongues plays in your experience.

Answer: I myself do not have the gift of the interpretation
of tongues, but I do know that glossolalia is not complete without there also being someone who can interpret the tongues. This
is very definitely a gift of God. The interpretations that I have
heard are wonderful. God will use this gift when God wishes
to give a direct message to the people, and there will always be
someone in the congregation who will be given the interpretation
by God—or it may be at times that God may give the interpretation to the same person that is speaking. Most people who
are born of the Spirit are able to interpret very accurately, while
others paraphrase very loosely. I have noted occasions where the
interpretation was not of the accurate type. The Holy Spirit will
then clarify the message with further instruction or translation.

Question 12: Have there been changes in your personal and
family life since you have spoken in tongues?

Answer: There has been a great change—my life is radically
changed as a result of this experience—a development quite to
be expected after a direct and personal encounter with the Holy
Spirit. I know this from personal experience and so does every
other child of God who belongs to him (our speaking in tongues
is our seal to prove we belong to Him). Christ is alive in us.
He walks with us and talks with us, He leads and guides, He
is our banker—He puts money in our pocket, He makes a $5
bill stretch into a $10 bill, He pulls us back from danger and
covers us from unknown dangers.

Questions 13 and 14: What part does tongue-speaking play
in your congregation? How has the congregation reacted to this
gift?

Answer: Rumors have been spread that the speaking in
tongues has caused a split in our congregation. The truth is

that those who have been prayed for that they might receive all that God has to offer have not caused any trouble. They are the finest and most cooperative group that one can ever hope to meet in this world. The split in our congregation has been caused by those who oppose the Holy Spirit, speak evil of his gifts, and are not satisfied to live by the Word alone, and are not willing to forgive those who desire to do what is right. Harmony in our church cannot be attained by opposing the Word of God and grieving the Holy Spirit.

Question 15: What can be done to ensure that tongue-speaking be used for the greatest possible mutual edification of all members of the church, both tongue-speakers and non-tongue-speakers?

Answer: There should be more tolerance. People who do speak in tongues should be left alone and not bothered by those who do not speak in tongues. Some people make fun of those who have this gift. There must be firmness in standing on the Word of God, and there must be opposition to those who speak as though Satan promotes the speaking in tongues. People should be urged to believe the Word of God in all its fullness.

Question 16: Are you aware of any abuses of the gifts of tongues? Is it possible to differentiate between the gift of the Spirit and so-called 'false prophecy"?

Answer: There can be abuses. We have had occasion to witness this phenomena both in scheduled religious services and in small gatherings, and have observed a large variety of manifestations (some convincingly genuine and others obviously feigned). Not all glossolalia appears directed by the Holy Spirit, but much by a desire to be accepted by congregations where the gift is held in esteem. There should always be an attempt to distinguish this, as the difference is fundamental. Through the gift of discernment it is possible to make this differentiation. There are rumors that tongues have been received through coaching, but this is not true so far as I know. Those who are speaking in tongues or have spoken in tongues seem to receive the gift immediately, or later on when they were alone with God. Hence it is not coaching which is effective but faith, prayer, the laying on of hands, and the Word in the use of tongues, and we pray that in every way we might be an example of true religion.

Question 17: What is the relationship between tongues and other charismatic gifts, e.g., prophecy, healing, interpretation, etc.? What other gifts of the Spirit do you have?

Answer: These are all gifts of God, conferred upon persons as God sees fit, and always for some special purpose that God has in mind for the person upon whom the gift is bestowed. The Bible says that tongues is one of the lesser gifts, and the greatest gift is the gift of love. Most people have only one gift of the Spirit, and a few people I know maybe have two gifts. I pray for receiving other gifts, but up to now, I have only the gift of tongues.

Question 18: Is there anything you can add which will help us understand the gift of tongues?

Answer: The question does come to mind as to how far the Holy Spirit will cooperate with a scientific inquiry based upon the world's knowledge and techniques. Martin Luther correctly stressed that "the just shall live by faith." I understand that your research has remained outside of any religious considerations—a manifest impossibility from the standpoint of a Spirit-filled Christian. Let me say that you can't take a supernatural blessing bestowed from God and bring it down to a common denominator or natural level. We have long conjectured upon the possibility of not merely recording the messages, but of measuring the source of the message just as radio and TV waves can be identified. However, again this may not be permitted because "His ways are past finding out," and this might not be of faith. May God fill you with the Spirit of Truth so that you do not lie, believe lies, nor spread them.

3

Historical Perspective: *How Much Has Glossolalia Been Practiced?*

The term *glossolalia* is derived from the Greek words *glossa* —the tongue, and *lalein*—to talk. Its literal meaning is to speak with the tongue, which is of course how everyone speaks. It has come to denote the experience in which a person seemingly speaks a language he has never learned, or a series of sounds not known to be speech of any group on earth. Webster's unabridged *Third New International Dictionary* definition begins: "ecstatic speech that is usually unintelligible to hearers," and the unabridged *Random House Dictionary* offers: "a prayer characterized chiefly by incomprehensible speech."

Glossolalia or speaking in tongues is not restricted to Christian experience. Ecstatic utterances of a divinely inspired nature are mentioned in early Egyptian writings. The oracles of Delphi, Dodona, and Epirus among many others, which laid claim to prophecy, sometimes through the spirits of the dead, appear to be related to glossolalia. Plato extolled "four kinds of irrational experience, the divine madness of love, prophecy, Dionysian ecstasy, and poetic intuition," and both Plutarch and Virgil recorded phenomena similar to glossolalia.

BIBLICAL REFERENCES

Glossolalists draw support for the religious content of their practice from several Old Testament passages. Isaiah 28:11,12 is often quoted.

> So it will be with barbarous speech and strange tongue
>   that this people will hear God speaking,
>   this people to whom he once said,
> 'This is true rest; let the exhausted have rest.
> This is repose,' and they refused to listen. [NEB]

Interestingly, Paul cites Isaiah 28:11 in I Corinthians 14:21 as evidence that ecstatic utterances are of questionable value to the Christian community. Because of the unintelligibility of glossolalia he urges the use of prophesy, which is communicable and involves the intelligence.

Because the Holy Spirit is thought to be the agent of ecstatic Christian speech references to the Spirit in the Psalms are considered relevant. Typical are:

Create in me a clean heart, O God, and renew a right spirit within me.

Cast me not away from thy presence; and take not thy holy spirit from me. [51:10, 11, KJV]

and

> Lord, thou hast examined me and knowest me. . . .
> Thou hast kept close guard before me and behind
>   and hast spread thy hand over me. . . . .
> Where can I escape from thy spirit?
>   Where can I flee from thy presence? [139:1, 5, 7, NEB]

Tongue-speakers also like to quote Joel 2:28,29. Peter uses this Old Testament scripture to validate the pentecostal experience (Acts 2:17,18) by identifying speaking in tongues with prophecy. But in this case the ecstatic speech was clearly understandable.

The major New Testament references to glossolalia appear in the Acts of the Apostles and in the writings of Paul. The second chapter of Acts records that on the day of Pentecost, when the Apostles were all gathered together in a house, "there appeared to them tongues like flames of fire, dispersed among them and resting on each one. And they were all filled with the Holy Spirit and began to talk in other tongues, as the Spirit gave them power of utterance" (Acts 2:3,4). A varied crowd of foreigners assembled and were astonished that the Apostles, all Galileans, spoke so that each could understand them in his own native language. This example of glossolalia is cited as the spontaneous ability to speak in a previously unknown language, although technically the testimony to the experience is in the ear of the auditor rather than in ability of the speaker.

Acts 10:44-46 tells of Gentiles having received the gift of the Holy Spirit, "speaking in tongues of ecstasy and acclaiming the greatness of God." It is difficult to determine whether the writer means intelligible or unintelligible glossalalia, or both, in this passage. But Paul may have been alluding to this type of experience when he says (in I Cor. 14:22—referring back to Joel 2:28), "Clearly then these 'strange tongues' are not intended as a sign for believers, but for unbelievers. . . ." At any rate in I Corinthians 12:10, 11 Paul explicitly recognizes both "the gift of ecstatic utterance of different kinds, and . . . the ability to interpret it" as a true work of the Spirit.

Glossolalia in current usage is not of the type described in Acts. In the past the ability has been claimed for some early Christian missionaries, but today there are no verified instances of a tongue-speaker having a foreign language at his command which he has not learned by the usual means. Rather, current practice resembles the I Corinthians type of glossolalia in which

no one, including the speaker, knows what he is saying. Unintelligible sounds are uttered, and a few persons, to whom is
attributed the "gift of interpretation," report that they are able
to discern the meaning of what is said.

EARLY CHURCH FATHERS

Data on glossolalia after the times of the Apostles are scarce
and frequently obscure. The picture is complicated. Glossolalia
is not clearly differentiated from the gift of prophecy[1]—a problem which also besets the New Testament material.

For instance Irenaeus, a church father writing in the last half
of the second century, mentions Peter's visit to Caesarea and
substitutes the word "prophesy" for the term "speaking in
tongues," and when listing the "gifts of the Holy Spirit" does
not mention glossolalia.

Montanus, a second-century deviate Christian preacher from
Phrygia, practiced glossolalia to proclaim the imminent end of
the world. His predictions proved false. His theology was
deemed heretical, but some present-day glossolalists quote
Montanus and his sect as valid exemplars of tongue-speaking.

After the first century there are only few references to glossolalia in Christian discourse. The lack of material on this subject has been interpreted in two ways. Some authorities believe
that the gift of tongues was insignificant in the development in
the early church. Others interpret the poverty of references to
the fact that, since glossolalia was easily misunderstood by non-
speakers, to divulge such a gift would arouse public hostility.

There is some question about the espousal of glossolalia by
Tertullian, a major shaper of western Christian doctrine during
the early years of the third century. Proponents of the validity of
glossolalia as a spiritual experience state that he was specific as

---

1. Morton T. Kelsey, *Tongue-Speaking: An Experiment in Spiritual Experience* (New York: Doubleday & Co., 1964), pp. 34, 35.

to its existence and real values. Other authorities emphasize the passing influence of Montanism on some of his writings and find the references rather less specific and sometimes even ambiguous.

Origen, writing in mid-third century, and Chrysostom a hundred years later both disparaged the accounts of glossolalia and claimed that if it had ever been a part of Christian practice, it was valid no longer.

Augustine of Hippo asserted in the early fifth century that speaking in tongues was a sign adapted to biblical times: "That thing was done for a betokening, and it passed away."[2] However, some scholars believe that he did in fact uphold the use of glossolalia and that it was still practiced in his lifetime, and they have attempted to document their claims. One recently credited Augustine with saying

We still do what the apostles did when they laid hands on the Samaritans and called down the Holy Spirit on them by the laying on of hands. It is expected that converts should speak with new tongues.[3]

Other scholars oppose this view.

It is evident that during the first few centuries of the Christian era speaking in tongues was regarded ambiguously by those whose lot it was to form the basic doctrine of the church.

THE MIDDLE AGES

The Middle Ages, a period noted for its deep interest in and commitment to events of wonder and mystery, reveal few recorded instances of glossolalia. Biographies of the great missionary saints of the time—Vincent Ferrer, Francis Xavier, and

---

2. *Homilies on the First Epistle of John,* VI, 10, in *Nicene and Post-Nicene Fathers,* First Series, edited by Philip Schaff and Henry Wace (Grand Rapids: Wm. B. Eerdmans Publishing Co., 1952), Vol. 7.

3. John L. Sherrill, *They Speak with Other Tongues.* London: Hodder and Stoughton Ltd., 1965.

Louis Bertrand—long perpetuated the notion that these individuals possessed the gift of tongues in the sense that they could speak existing foreign languages of which they had little or no knowledge. They supposedly had been given this gift in order to convert the non-European pagan peoples of the world to Christianity.

More careful study of the facts indicates that the biographers were subject to the power of the myth. Xavier, for example, in his letters to his superiors and other associates, told of his difficulties in attempting to master such Oriental languages as Japanese. He wrote that he used both sign language and interpreters to assist him in preaching the gospel in Japan and China.

POST-REFORMATION ERA

In 1685, Louis XIV of France revoked the Edict of Nantes and called upon the Hugenots to return to the Roman Catholic Church. He reinforced his urgings with severe persecution, and the Hugenots experienced such phenomena as "strange sounds in the air; the sound of a trumpet and a harmony of voices."[4] A twelve-year-old girl, Isabeau Vincent, was the first to receive these manifestations of the Spirit; she was followed by numerous others, by some reports as many as eight thousand in one province alone. Most of those affected were children—they were called the "little prophets of Cevennes," and the episodes continued until 1711. The little prophets, like the Montanists of the second century, proclaimed the imminent coming of Christ and the end of the world.

The Jansenists, a Catholic Holiness sect which came into being in the 1730's as a counterforce to the barren spirit and lax morality of the church, practiced glossolalia. Their spiritual

4. R. Heath, "The Little Prophets of the Cevennes," *Contemporary Review* 49 (January, 1886): 117.

utterances were unintelligible to both the speaker and the hearer.

Several splinter groups among the early Quakers espoused glossolalia as a significant religious experience, one of the best known being the so-called Ranters in England. According to some authorities, George Fox and other leaders avoided the practice. Other scholars, however, allege that Fox was the originator of it.

Glossolia seems to have been even more widespread in England during the early years of the nineteenth century. Edward Irving, pastor of a Presbyterian church in London, reports hearing of several instances of tongue-speaking that took place in Scotland. For instance Mary Campbell, a pious invalid, began one day to speak in sounds unlike any language she knew or had heard. A fellow countryman in another city, James Mac-Donald, had the same experience and upon hearing of Mary Campbell wrote to her, telling her to rise from her sickbed. This she did, and lived a healthy life thereafter. Irving, impressed by this incident encouraged his congregation to pray for the gift of tongues. Glossolalia broke out among his flock, and he founded a new sect called the Catholic Apostolic Church. He died in 1834, but a few of his faithful followers continued the practice of tongue-speaking for about forty years; the sect finally went out of existence.

Glossolalia also appeared in Sweden, Norway, and the United States during the early part of the nineteenth century. In the Scandinavian countries most of the participants were young children, sometimes only four years of age, as had been the case in Cevennes. In England and the United States mainly adults were involved. The speech manifested was an unintelligible "language" often interpreted by another, spiritually adept member of the congregation.

The Church of the Latter-day Saints—popularly known as Mormons—was founded in 1830 by Joseph Smith in New York. Belief in gifts of the Spirit was one of its articles of faith.

Emphasis was placed on "the gifts of tongues, prophecy, revelation, visions, healing, interpretation of tongues, etc."[5]

Scattered references are found indicating that glossolalia occurred in Orthodox Russia in the nineteenth century. In 1880 in the Armenian village of Kara Kala an outbreak of tongue-speaking is reported, mainly involving Presbyterians. In 1900 this group left Kara Kala and settled in Los Angeles. They practiced their religion as a small isolated sect for some years in the New World until a day in 1906, when by chance one of their members passed an old building on Azusa Street. He was astounded to hear from within the familiar sounds of people speaking in tongues and worshiping in a manner similar to his own group. Thus two streams of Pentecostalism came together.

THE TWENTIETH CENTURY

The Pentecostal church in the United States may be said to have begun with Charles Parham, a Methodist minister who in 1900 started a Bible school in Topeka, Kansas, with the intention of revitalizing the Christian experience. Five years later he opened a second school in Houston, Texas. One of the students at this institution was W. J. Seymour, a Negro minister.

Seymour began preaching on the gifts of the Holy Spirit, particularly the gift of tongues. After one such sermon in Los Angeles, the elders of the church found this material unacceptable and locked the church against him. Seymour then preached in an old lodging house where he was living, until the exuberance of the congregation literally brought down the roof of the building. In 1906 he moved to an old but large and sturdy building at 312 Azusa Street—noted above—which became the center of Pentecostalism. The revival meeting on Azusa Street in Los Angeles lasted for three years and was attended by per-

5. J. H. Beadle, *Life in Utah: Mysteries and Crimes of Mormonism* (Philadelphia: National Publishing Co., 1870), pp. 321-23.

sons from all over the world. When they returned home they founded similar Pentecostal groups there.

The background of the Pentecostal churches was the Holiness movement which began in the United States after the Civil War. The Holiness sects, already committed to individual conversion and constant, intense efforts to become sanctified, were led naturally to a third tenet: the "second baptism" of the Holy Spirit, which would render the first two doctrines more meaningful and possible. The movement differed from orthodox Protestantism in three basic ways: (1) it was fundamentalist, holding to literal translation of the Bible and denial of Darwin's theories; (2) it insisted on the necessity of individual conversion, by contrast with the doctrine of Christian nurture which taught that a child raised according to Christian ideals would *ipso facto* be a Christian; and (3) it emphasized the moral perfection of the individual as the mission of the church, rather than social reforms.

The Pentecostal doctrine is fundamentalist with the added belief that "the *full* New Testament baptism in the Spirit was made manifest by the *glossolalia,* and that it was the will of God to pour out His Spirit in this manner upon all flesh."[6] It soon gained thousands of followers, and there are in the United States today at least twenty-six sects which claim to be Pentecostal.[7] The largest is the Assemblies of God, with the Church of God in Christ and the Church of God second and third, respectively. Others are: the International Church of the Foursquare Gospel, the Pentecostal Church of God in America, the Apostolic Overcoming Holy Church of God, the Pentecostal Holiness Church, and the Pentecostal Assemblies of the World. It has been esti-

6. Carl Brumback, *What Meaneth This?* (Springfield, Mo.: Gospel Publishing House. 1947), p. 92.

7. Klaude Kendrick, *The Promise Fulfilled: A History of the Modern Pentecostal Movement* (Springfield, Mo.: Gospel Publishing House, 1961), pp. 68-70.

mated that there are two million members of these and similar Pentecostal churches in the United States alone.[8]

THE CURRENT GENERATION

In 1960 there was a new surge of interest in glossolalia, this time crossing many denominational lines—Lutheran, Episcopal, Presbyterian, and so on. This new outbreak has been referred to as "denominational Pentecostalism"[9] or "neo-Pentecostalism."

The first instance which was accorded widespread publicity involved Father Dennis F. Bennett, pastor of St. Mark's Episcopal Church in Van Nuys, California. One Sunday Father Bennett described from the pulpit his own experience with glossolalia. An associate priest left the chancel in protest. But then about seventy members of the congregation witnessed that they also had had glossolalic experiences. Numerous incidents of the phenomenon were then published, which occurred in such diverse places as the Episcopal Church of the Advent in Alice, Texas and the universities of Yale, Harvard, Princeton, Stanford, and UCLA. The Roman Catholic *Messenger,* discussing the subject, stated:

Charism comes from a Greek word meaning literally a gift of love. As used by theologians, it describes a special talent freely bestowed by the Holy Spirit. In this vein we must today recognize the existence of charisms for a balanced view of the Church, seeing them not as accidental additions, but as part of its nature.[10]

One of the best-known names in Pentecostal and neo-Pentecostal circles is that of David du Plessis, a South African minister who was among those who brought the message back to his

8. Sherrill, *op. cit.,* p. 15.

9. James W. Hoffman, "Speaking in Tongues, 1963," *Presbyterian Life,* September 1, 1963, p. 16.

10. *Catholic Messenger,* November 7, 1963.

own country from Azusa Street in Los Angeles. He preached, edited a Pentecostal newspaper, and became executive secretary of the Pentecostal Fellowships of South Africa. In 1949 he became secretary-general of the World Conference of Pentecostal Fellowships. There had been from the beginning of the movement a wide and bitter rift between the Pentecostal churches and the traditional denominations, with little true communication between them. Du Plessis came to the conclusion that he had been called to make an effort to break down the barrier between the Pentecostal and the traditional churches. He sought to work with the World Council of Churches and was subsequently dismissed from his position with the Assemblies of God. Nevertheless he has continued his ecumenical work.

By 1964 nearly every large Protestant organization, including the mission boards, had had episodes involving glossolalia.[11] While the lower economic strata of society have traditionally filled the ranks of Holiness sects and Pentecostal churches, the current movement is among the wealthier, most highly educated congregations of the Baptist, Presbyterian, Lutheran, Methodist, Episcopal, and Congregationalist churches (now United Church of Christ). These glossolalists tend to be discreet about their practice. In his book published in 1964 Sherrill remarks that although his research produced numerous replies from ministers and laymen who had experienced tongue-speaking, every one asked that he remain anonymous.

More recently many accounts of glossolalia have been published. For instance, an article in the *Saturday Evening Post* of May 16, 1964 drew to public attention the meetings held by the United Presbyterian Church of Upper Octoraro, Pennsylvania, which attracted hundreds of persons, including ministers of other denominations. Faith healings are also reported to have taken place in the course of these meetings. The Trinity Epis-

11. McCandlish Phillips, "And There Appeared to Them Tongues of Fire," *Saturday Evening Post,* May 16, 1964, p. 32.

copal Church in Wheaton, Illinois has also been a focal point in articles on glossolalia.

The Blessed Trinity Society was organized in the late 1950's and dedicated to spreading the word about glossolalia, chiefly through its (now defunct) quarterly publication, *Trinity*. It was the hope of many Pentecostal leaders that if glossolalia could be accepted as a normal religious practice, many hitherto isolated sects and individuals would be given courage to make their experiences public.

In the 1970's there have been numerous tongue-speakers in the Jesus movement. And the charismatic development among Roman Catholics has included several thousand persons known to speak in tongues.

The neo-Pentecostal movement is at present quite widespread; its basic tenets seem to be identical with those of older Pentecostal sects. They are that glossolalia is a true gift of the Holy Spirit, and that it is "the necessary evidence that one has received the baptism of the Spirit."[12] The major difference lies in the emotional approach, in that the neo-Pentecostalists maintain a separation between their usual church services and the meetings in which tongue-speaking is practiced, whereas the Pentecostalists identify tongue-speaking with services and feel that these amount only to "tarrying"—that is, awaiting the will of God— if no one speaks forth in tongues.

In any event, glossolalia looms on the contemporary religious scene as a controversial but very real phenomenon involving many thousands of sincere individuals.

12. Anthony A. Hoekema, *What About Tongue-Speaking?* (Grand Rapids Wm. B. Eerdmans Publishing Co., 1966), p. 48.

4

Seven Theories

Much of the current literature tends to regard glossolalia as a true expression of a spiritual gift, closely akin to, if not identical with, the phenomenon of Pentecost as related in the New Testament book of Acts. Some researchers however are inclined to treat it as an almost purely psychological manifestation.

This chapter summarizes the views of seven authors on the spiritual and psychological factors related to glossolalia.

LAURENCE CHRISTENSON

Laurence Christenson does not employ psychological categories to explain glossolalia. In his book *Speaking in Tongues,* he affirms that it is totally a spiritual experience. He believes that the phenomenon "involves a supernatural manifestation of the Holy Spirit which is clearly spoken of in the Bible."[1] Christenson, pastor of Trinity Lutheran Church in San Pedro, California and a leading figure in the neo-Pentecostal movement, is critical of those who downgrade glossolalia as a fad or as mere emotionalism. He admits of no possibility that true tongue-speaking could be a sign of mental instability. He states that in

1. Laurence Christenson, *Speaking in Tongues* (Minneapolis: Bethany Fellowship, Publishers, 1968), p. 18.

recent years "thousands and perhaps millions" of Christians of every denomination have testified that they have received this "gift of the Spirit," and that it has resulted in a rebirth of faith for many (p. 15 and *passim*). He feels that in an era so often characterized as post-Christian, this resurgence of the Spirit should be neither ignored nor denigrated.

Christenson interprets biblical speaking in tongues as an act neither of teaching nor of instruction, but rather of worship and adoration. He believes that this is also true of present-day manifestations. Neither in cases where the language is unknown nor where it is at least unknown to the speaker, does the latter "control" the meaning of what he is saying. Others in the congregation may interpret, but this is also considered a gift from the Holy Ghost. Christenson asserts that the dictionary definition of language—"Any means, vocal or otherwise, of expressing or communicating feeling or thought"—also accurately defines glossolalia.

Christenson does not consider that a glossolalist is either "hysterical" or "ecstatic." Although possibly the hearer is described in the Bible as "ecstatic (existanto)—Acts 2:7, or amazed (exestesan)—Acts 10:45" (p. 24), the terms are nowhere applied to biblical speakers.

GEORGE BARTON CUTTEN

The many psychological explanations of glossolalia that have been advanced over the years are discussed in detail by George Barton Cutten (chapter 9, *passim*), in *Speaking with Tongues*, which has been the standard work in this field since it was written in 1927.[2] But Cutten makes the point that such explanations are at best only partial, since to name a psychological condition does not explain it, and it does not necessarily exclude the possibility of divine causation.

2. George Barton Cutten, *Speaking with Tongues: Historically and Psychologically Considered* (New Haven: Yale University Press, 1927).

Cutten states that a *modern* (1927) psychological interpretation of glossolalia stresses that the person who speaks in tongues must be considered to be experiencing a state of "personal disintegration in which the verbo-motive centers of the subject are obedient to subconscious impulses" (p. 160). The take-over by the subconscious is similar to that manifested in automatic writing and in various kinds of hallucinatory experiences. The mental excitement which produces glossolalia also often coincides with visions and auditory hallucinations. However, Cutten recognizes that the desire of some Christians to experience all of the gifts promised by Christ has been a continuing one.

Glossolalia as a psychological condition, says Cutten, is usually ascribed to hysteria, ecstasy, or catalepsy. Hysteria is a condition in which the individual is extremely susceptible to suggestion and any sensations he feels are exaggerated. The ecstatic condition by contrast seems to be so dominated by some central idea that there is suspension of sensation similar to the cataleptic state.

Although catalepsy is usually characterized by rigidity of the body, a symptom rarely present in those who speak in tongues, some psychologists have characterized glossolalists as cataleptic. However, in the form of catalepsy which some authorities feel closely resembles the condition of tongue-speakers, the person affected afterward remembers any visions or auditory hallucinations experienced while unconscious.

Cutten does not agree with the opinion that glossolalia is a form of hypnotism. It is true that certain requisites for successful inducement of the hypnotic state are also present in tongue-speaking, such as rapport between the subject and the leader, uniformity of perception, fixation of the subject's attention, and suggestion. But Cutten believes that the experience of hypnotism differs fundamentally from that of glossolalia.

He defines the various degrees of speaking in tongues as "1) inarticulate sounds, 2) articulate sounds which simulate words, and 3) fabricated or coined words" (p. 169), and ascribes them to an abnormal mental condition of the speaker. He asserts that it has been well documented that in cases when a speaker has used a foreign language formerly unknown to him the speaker has in reality been sufficiently exposed to the language to speak it; it existed in his subconscious and was brought out under abnormal conditions, without volition on his part. Cutten cites a number of thoroughly investigated cases which support this theory.

ANTHONY A. HOEKEMA

What About Tongue Speaking? is a biblical and theological evaluation of glossolalia by the professor of systematic theology at Calvin Theological Seminary. The author does not believe that the phenomenon is divinely inspired, yet he states that there is much of value in the experience. He concedes that it has struck a deep spiritual response in many persons.

Hoekema cites V. Raymond Edman to substantiate his views. Edman argues that there are only three possible explanations of the phenomenon: (1) it is a gift of the Spirit, (2) it is a snare of the devil, or (3) it is an abnormal psychological condition.[3] Because glossolalia is not always a religious experience, but arises in a variety of individuals and groups subjected to strongly repressed emotional forces, Hoekema inclines to the view that it is a psychological phenomenon which is readily produced and easily understood.

But the evidence that many persons, especially among the neo-Pentecostals, have affirmed a "true spiritual rebirth" as the result of their speaking in tongues is for him a major difficulty. He concludes therefore that resurgence of faith results from conditions preceding and accompanying glossolalia. The hours

---

3. V. Raymond Edman, "Divine or Devilish?" *Christian Herald* 87 (May 1964): 14-16, quoted in Anthony A. Hoekema, *What About Tongue-Speaking?* (Grand Rapids: Wm. B. Eerdmans Publishing Co., 1966), p. 126.

spent in earnest meditation and prayer, the heartfelt desire to be closer to God, cannot help but produce a more fervent and perfect "spiritual harmony." Glossolalia itself is irrelevant to the rebirth of faith.

MORTON T. KELSEY

Morton T. Kelsey, rector (in 1961) of St. Luke's Episcopal Church in Monrovia, California, summarizes four different evaluations of glossolalia as follows: (1) it is a psychological abnormality or demonic possession (interchangeable from some points of view), (2) we do not know what it is—the original experience of Pentecost and related experiences have never been correctly interpreted, (3) speaking in tongues was useful in the early days of the church but is no longer of value, or (4) it is a spiritual gift, as valid today as in the times of the Apostles and given directly by the Holy Spirit.

Kelsey states that his research clearly shows glossolalia to be different in both kind and quality from either an ecstatic, hysterical experience or an innocuous release of strong religious emotions. He is very much interested in Freud's theory of the unconscious and in Jung's of the collective unconscious. He sees in the latter especially an explanation and validation of glossolalia.

Kelsey feels that if religion is a viable part of an individual's life, contact with the world of the "Spirit" can and often will be achieved. Openness to religious experience is frequently the hallmark of the individual who seeks closer union with God through tongue-speaking. The same openness to psychic reality, Kelsey believes, also results in faith healing, both of the mind and of the body.[4]

Kelsey discusses five views of glossolalia as a psychologically

4. Morton T. Kelsey, *Tongue-Speaking: An Experiment in Spiritual Experience* (New York: Doubleday & Co., 1961), pp. 192 *et seq.*

caused phenonemon: i.e., as (1) a manifestation of schizophrenia, (2) a form of hysteria, (3) a result of hypnotism, (4) a case of autosuggestion, and (5) an exalted memory based on repression (p. 210).

He reports some authorities as holding that tongue-speaking is a schizophrenic manifestation because the speaker allows himself to be possessed—or dispossessed—by the contents of his unconscious. It exhibits a typical schizophrenic pattern. Kelsey disagrees with this evaluation because the tongue-speaker suffers no damage to his ego and remains clearly able to differentiate between reality and unreality, both before and after the experience. A person already mentally ill might be unable to recover from the experience of tongue-speaking; however it would not be the fault of tongue-speaking per se, for such a victim would be unable to withstand any sort of strong assault on his ego. Kelsey does not believe that there is any causal relation between tongue-speaking and schizophrenia.

The theory that glossolalia is a form of hysteria is held by many workers in the field. Kelsey disagrees; while stating that both hysteria and tongue-speaking obviously arise in the unconscious, he sees no other connection. Hysteria is an illness which harms the mind and sometimes the body; glossolalia seems to result in an increased ability to cope with reality, both material and spiritual.

With regard to hypnotism Kelsey's views are similar to those of Hoekema, recognizing the fact that both hypnotism and speaking in tongues can open the mind to the unconscious. Here, says Kelsey, the likeness ceases.

The theory that glossolalia is a form of autosuggestion he dismisses out of hand as having little pertinence, for he thinks it extremely doubtful that an individual can "autosuggest himself into a transforming religious experience" (p. 211). And exalted memory, he observes, offers no explanation as to what might trigger the experience. Nor does that theory really explain the resulting spiritual value so often associated with glossolalia.

Kelsey propounds two additional psychological explanations of the experience of tongue-speaking: one based on its similarity to dreams in providing avenues of meaningful contact with the inner world of the spirit; the other on its similarity to visions. Both are contacts with psychic reality.

Glossolalia is a significant psychological and religious phenomenon, according to Kelsey, best understood in relation to the Jungian theory of the collective unconscious.

JAMES N. LAPSLEY AND JOHN H. SIMPSON

Lapsley and Simpson's article, "Speaking in Tongues," appeared in two parts in *Pastoral Psychology* and is concerned with the psychological significance of the phenomenon. The authors, professors at Princeton Theological Seminary, treat glossolalia from a psychological standpoint as psychomotor behavior with similarities to trance states, somnambulism, mediumship, and automatic writing. They advance the theory that individuals who have a deep need for personal security and emotional expression provide the bulk of those engaged in the neo-Pentecostal movement. Leaders are drawn from the ever-increasing number of ministers and clergymen in all denominations who have found themselves frustrated and anxious about their function and purpose in the traditional church.[5]

Speaking in tongues does indeed serve as a "singular emotional outlet." Several in-depth studies of tongue-speaking Pentecostals indicate that they are very troubled people; they exhibit more anxiety and personality instability than non-Pentecostals or non-tongue-speaking Pentecostals.

Neo-Pentecostals often emphasize the positive mental health

5. James N. Lapsley and John H. Simpson, "Speaking in Tongues: Token of Group Acceptance and Divine Approval," Parts I and II, *Pastoral Psychology*, May, 1964; September, 1964. This reference is to Part I, p. 52.

aspects of the phenomenon. Pentecostals do not. Carl Jung's theory of the collective unconscious figures largely in the neo-Pentecostals' concept of the meaning or source of glossolalia, and as we have seen, Morton Kesley also espouses this view. It is used to explain how a person can speak in a known tongue of which he has, and could have had, no knowledge, or in a tongue not recognized as any language but which might well be an unknown language either of the past or the present.

Lapsley and Simpson, in attempting to define the phenomenon in psychological terms, liken it to the form of automatism found in trance states and sleepwalking, because all or nearly all the voluntary muscles are dissociated from conscious control. Automatisms are considered to provide an escape valve for deep-seated conflicts within the individual.

Lapsley and Simpson declare that the total experience of glossolalia enables the tongue-speaker to express his feelings without ambivalence. This accounts for the overwhelming sensations of joy and release so often reported.

The authors are convinced by their research that emphasis on the demonic seems to be essential to both the Pentecostal and neo-Pentecostal movements. Tongue-speakers, say Lapsley and Simpson, apparently attain the same release from inner tensions as did ancients who were "possessed of the devil," with the advantage that glossolalia is not painful nor physically exhausting, contrary to the classical paroxysmal demon-possession (Part II, p. 19).

These authors consider that the practice of glossolalia includes a self-aggrandizing, narcissistic component. But they do not think that it hastens or causes a permanent disintegration of the personality but rather believe that due to the lessening of inner conflict the practice may in some cases be beneficial.

They are essentially ambivalent about the positive and negative effects of the practice. They feel that it does help some people reduce their inner conflicts and cope more adequately with the world. But the element of self-aggrandizement leads some to overemphasize their "specialness," isolating them along with their peer group from the mainstream of society.

The authors by stating that they consider glossolalia to be neither meaningless and infantile babble, nor yet a direct conversation with God, but rather "a dissociative expression of truncated personality development" (Part II, p. 24), in effect hold it to be a compartmentalized bit of behavior of an immature person.

WAYNE E. OATES

Wayne E. Oates is professor at Southern Baptist Theological Seminary. Intellectualization, institutionalization, and sophistication all result in the repression of deep religious feelings by many people, writes Oates in "A Socio-Psychological Study of Glossolalia." If these emotions finally break through it is understandable that the first attempts at communicating them sound like babble. However, individuals who overemphasize the glossolalic experience and become isolated from society because they feel unique may be considered psychopathological. Since not all tongue-speakers follow this pattern, no generalizations can be made as to the mental health of glossolalics.

Oates's treatise deals with studies of children's language and attempts to correlate these studies with glossolalia as "a child-like form of language."[6]

What some authorities call "infantile babble" is more scientifically described as similar to the second or parataxic phase of an infant's attempts to communicate. During this period the toddler repeats sounds which are meaningless to the listener but satis-

6. Wayne E. Oates, "A Socio-Psychological Study of Glossolalia," in Frank Stagg, E. Glenn Hinson, and Wayne E. Oates, *Glossolalia: Tongue Speaking in Biblical, Historical, and Psychological Perspective* (New York and Nashville: Abingdon Press, 1967), p. 78.

fying to the child. Another speech pattern typical of this level of development involves "dual or collective monologues."[7] The youngster still does not make sense in his speech, but is stimulated by the presence of another person or persons who are not included in the monologue or expected to respond to it. Oates believes that this accurately describes the phenomenon of glossolalia.

The distortions of speech which appear at this time are submerged by the child as he matures. According to Oates, these distortions reappear in tongue-speaking; as the individual tries to verbalize long-repressed religious convictions for the first time, he reverts to an early stage of communicative skill.

In discussing the possible connection between glossolalia and mental illness, Oates examines various mental states in which voluntary muscles are controlled by the unconscious. He refers to Lapsley and Simpson's characterization of glossolalia as a form of dissociation.

Sleep is one such mental stage; sexual orgasm is another. Relaxation of conscious control also occurs normally in socially acceptable mass or mob activity; for instance, at sports events or in lynching and rioting, relaxation takes an excessive form. Relaxation is attained in psychiatric practice by hypnosis, psychoanalysis, chemotherapy (sodium amytal, tranquilizers, etc), and electroconvulsive and insulin-convulsive therapy.

This book also questions the reasons for the present resurgence of the practice of glossolalia and for its appearance in different social strata than before. Some churchmen ascribe it to the renewed activity of the Holy Spirit. Oates believes it to be a breakthrough of deeply felt but long pent-up passions, which find expression in sounds unintelligible to the listener but meaningful to the speaker. Oates asserts that tongue-speakers tend to have weak egos, confused identities, high anxiety levels, and generally unstable personalities. Neo-Pentecostals particularly are often

7. Jean Piaget, *The Language and Thought of the Child* (New York: Meridian Books, 1955), pp. 87, 88.

members of the affluent middle class, professionals or quasi-professionals, suffering from the emotional deprivation common to our times. Sometimes individuals of this socio-economic level try to "break through" their loneliness by means of alcohol and/or drugs. Speaking in tongues, Oates feels, provides a form of breaking through which allows the psychically ill to communicate their deep and too-long-repressed religious emotions in a socially acceptable form.

JOHN L. SHERRILL

They Speak with Other Tongues is a personal account of the experience of glossolalia.[8] John Sherrill, a reporter and writer on the staff of *Guideposts* magazine, begins his story with a series of events which occurred during a serious illness. Although a practicing Christian all his life, he was then for the first time overcome by a deeply emotional consciousness of Christ. From it he dates his gradual involvement with glossolalia.

His initial "encounter with Christ" in a hospital room left a spiritual exaltation but eventually began to fade. Then he met Harold Bredesen, at that time pastor of the First Reformed Church in Mount Vernon, New York, and a leader in the neo-Pentecostal movement. Bredesen told Sherrill of his own experiences and Sherrill was inspired to undertake in-depth research into a religious interpretation of glossolalia with particular reference to the Pentecostal sects.

He began his study by acquainting himself with members and small groups within traditional churches who were practicing tongue-speaking. He was struck by the element of secrecy which at that time surrounded their activities, but found it could be accounted for by the hostility of pastors and other members of their congregations to the phenomenon and its practitioners. Sherrill does not comment on the psychological theory which explains secrecy as a vital part of the mystique of an in-group.

8. London: Hodder and Stoughton Ltd., 1965.

In 1960 Sherrill heard a sermon by Father Bennett of St. Mark's Episcopal Church in Van Nuys, California, in which the preacher witnessed to his own experience with tongue-speaking and the charismatic renewal movement in which he played a decisive role.

Sherrill's highly colored personal narrative emphasizes his belief that glossolalia is a gift of the Holy Spirit, one which has a firm historical background and is again assuming the importance it had in the early days of the church. Sherrill sees the practice as a response to the needs of modern Christians in an essentially godless society.

His description of his own experience closely parallels the clinical exposition stated by Lapsley and Simpson in psychological terms as a "singular emotional outlet." Sherrill observes his own gradual loss of self-awareness, his cognizance that he was "speaking" in unintelligible grunts. He emphasizes the deep inner sense of joy and satisfaction that he received in the process. He states that he felt at peace with warring factions inside himself and experienced psychic healing. Faith healing is covered at length in the book, since Sherrill feels it to be closely bound to speaking in tongues.

Sherrill, who views glossolalia in a purely religious context, does not advance psychological explanations for the phenomenon, but his experiences and the language in which he expresses himself closely parallel the psychological explanations by other writers. They are particularly similar to the Jungian theory of an experienced psychic reality which somehow "fused together the antagonistic elements of the individual personality. . . . These warring opposites within the total personality . . . came to reconcilation and peace."

Sherrill is interested in what he calls the "group mind." He believes that "intimate, sustaining group-fellowship" is a distinguishing feature of glossolalia.

5

An Empirical Investigation

If you should ever try to imitate someone speaking in a foreign language, you will discover that you soon run out of sounds. You will run dry. Most people can imitate a strange language for only a few sentences, then the easy syllables become obvious, and stammering and hesitation take the place of fluency.

Tongue-speakers can go on almost endlessly in a fluid, easy manner. They never seem to be grasping for a new syllable. Because their performance cannot be duplicated by non-tongue-speakers, even with strenuous conscious effort, a psychologist must say that glossolalia is not completely under the conscious control of the person who speaks in tongues.

Study of what behavioral scientists call ego psychology and of the practice of hypnosis have helped to explain the phenomena involved.

EGO PSYCHOLOGY

When a tongue-speaker is able to continue pronouncing such phrases as "aish nay gum nay tayo" indefinitely, what controls his tongue? Such language differs radically from purposefully motivated sentences like "I want a drink of water," or even an exclamation like "My what a beautiful day!" These sentences are clearly under the control of the ego; "aish nay gum nay tayo" is not.

The ego is the conscious agent by which choices and judgments are made. In glossolalia conscious control is not exercised in the usual way. One of the major aims of the study of tongue-speaking is to determine the relationship between ego control and glossolalia. When control is reduced, the subject experiences regression. Typical examples are the ten-year-old who begins to suck his thumb after being scolded, or the tense businessman who finds himself stroking the soft leather of his chair during a harried confrontation with a client.

When Norman Rockwell does a *Saturday Evening Post* cover, his ego control is very precise. But when Jackson Pollock dripped paint "randomly" over a huge canvas stretched out on the floor, his ego was not entirely in control. This is an example of "regression in the service of the ego." So, on another level, is singing in the bathtub! Dipping into the unconscious sometimes produces unusually creative effects.

An important question in the study of glossolalia is how a tongue-speaker is able to call upon his unconscious so that he can fluently produce unintelligible speech and still maintain enough ego control to drive a truck on an interstate highway.

A concurrent question is what conditions must exist to induce unconscious speech. Does it have any relationship to mental health? Using Freudian terminology, the psycho-analyst Heinz Hartmann, gives a theoretical description of ego control useful in understanding the experience of glossolalia. He writes:

. . . occasional regressions in the service of the ego can be tolerated by the adult ego if its functions are unimpaired. We also know that the healthy ego, for certain purposes, has to be able to abandon itself to the id (as in sleep or in sexual intercourse). There are also other less well studied situations in which the ego itself induces a temporary discarding of some of its most highly differentiated functions. To do this, not only without impairment of normal function but even to its benefit, is an achievement that has to learned. The child, up to a certain age is not capable of using this mechanism, or feels threatened by its attempted use.[1]

In *My Fair Lady,* when Professor Higgins has his protégé practice saying, "The rain in Spain falls mainly on the plain," she is attempting a "highly differentiated ego function," as Dr. Hartmann might describe it. On the other hand, the tongue-speaker who says "oneeo romo goro agaranee," has temporarily discarded some of his ego functioning.

HYPNOSIS

There is a similarity between what happens when people are induced to speak in tongues and the process of hypnotism. When I hypnotize someone, I begin by saying to my subject, "Lie back . . . shut your eyes . . . relax . . . breath deeply . . . and listen to the sounds of your breathing. As you relax, you can feel yourself getting tired and drowsy . . ."

In the dimly lit fireside room of the First Presbyterian Church, a small circle of members quietly listened to their pastor say, "The Lord is in your presence . . . . He is with you now . . . open yourself to him . . . empty yourself of all other thoughts . . . wait upon him . . . let all your anxieties flow out of you. . . . The Lord wants to give you the gift of his Holy Spirit . . . . Open your mouth, and he will give you utterance . . . ."

The standard reference work by Ernest Hilgard, *Hypnotic Susceptibility,* makes it clear that hypnosis and glossolalia are induced in a similar manner. "The hypnotist has essentially a two-pronged strategy: that of sensory deprivation and that of developing a 'special' kind of relationship, i.e., a regressive transference based on a relationship to the hypnotist as in some

1. Heinz Hartmann, *Essays on Ego Psychology* (New York: International Universities Press, 1965), p. 177.

sense a parent substitute."[2] The following example of such a relationship is given: "the subject . . . is invited to permit himself to fall voluntarily, to see what it feels like to let go. A subject who steps back to break his fall, as though some part of him lacks confidence that he will be caught, almost invariably turns out to be a poor (hypnotic) subject" (p. 101). It seems possible that this same trust, or the lack of it, enables some persons, but not others, to begin to speak in tongues.

FIVE RESEARCH HYPOTHESES

As Dr. Qualben and I began to penetrate the psychology of glossolalia, five hypotheses emerged as particularly worthy of further study.

1. Knowing that one had to be able to follow a leader's suggestions in order to be hypnotized, we wished to determine whether glossolalists were more submissive, suggestible, and dependent—more able to follow a leader—than non-tongue-speakers.

2. We endeavored to test the theory that glossolalists probably initiated their speech while thinking about, and feeling emotionally close to, some kindly leader, who was also strong and masterful.

3. We also decided to investigate the phenomenon of glossolalia as an example of "regression in the service of the ego," for our initial research showed that it provided release from conflict and tension, and allowed a person to feel less depressed. The subject in a successful hypnosis having "let go" also feels more relaxed.

4. We guessed that the emotional benefits of tongue-speaking did not last for a long period of time. Once the novelty of the experience had disappeared, we thought that glossolalia would

2. Ernest Hilgard, *Hypnotic Susceptibility* (New York: Harcourt, Brace & World, 1965), p. 25.

become routine and that the glossolalist would settle back into his former emotional condition.

5. It became evident that it was of utmost importance to learn how linguists appraised the "languages" spoken by glossolalists. We had heard many stories about the identification of glossolalia as an extant, if obscure, tongue. The typical story is that a foreign visitor to a meeting at which glossolalia is practiced cries out, "That's my language!" However, in the history of tongue-speaking there are no scientifically confirmed recordings of anyone speaking in a foreign language which he had never learned. The events of Pentecost and the stories of the missionary saints cannot be validated from a scientific point of view. Other reports are generally thirdhand accounts.

THE RESEARCH PROCEDURE

Armed with these five hypotheses, we interviewed in depth and gave psychological tests to twenty glossolalists and twenty nonglossolalists. All the subjects were active members of mainline Protestant congregations. The work was started during the summer after our initial research. Every subject volunteered freely to take part in the study. The twenty glossolalists were termed Group A and the nonglossolalists Group B for research purposes.

The two groups were equated for religiosity. This was defined as the extent of a person's involvement in the church's activities. It included participation in worship services, membership on church boards and committees, and the verbalized concern of a person for the life and growth of his congregation. By all of these standards the members of both groups A and B would be considered "very religious." Less easily quantified, but of great significance, was the individual's "spirituality." Here we could only note that the members of both groups seemed equally engrossed in prayer, Bible study, and "the things of God." Next, the groups were equated for age, sex, and marital status; also for educational attainment. A small imbalance arose because it was not possible to obtain three non-tongue-speakers who had had three years of postcollege education to balance three clergymen tongue-speakers who had. Omitting the clergymen, the median numbers of years of education for each group was fourteen.

Three procedures were used to evaluate the two groups: (1) Each person was engaged by Dr. Qualben in a structured psychiatric interview. (2) I administered four psychological tests to each person. They were: the Rorschach Test, the Draw-A-Person Test, the Thematic Apperception Test, and the Minnesota Multiphasic Personality Inventory. (3) Each tongue-speaker recorded a sample of his tongue-speaking on tape. He performed this task in either Dr. Qualben's or my presence for two or three minutes. He voluntarily terminated the speech when he felt that an adequate sample had been given. Three subjects declined to record their speech, because they felt that such a procedure was out of keeping with the private, meditative nature of speaking in tongues.

RESULTS OF THE RESEARCH

Our research corroborated Hypothesis 1: that glossolalists are more submissive, suggestible, and dependent in the presence of authority figures than non-tongue-speakers.

Hypothesis 2 was also confirmed. They always thought about some benevolent authority person when they began to speak in tongues. Glossolalists, in other words, do initiate their speech in the presence of such a figure, whether in reality or fantasy.

Research on the third hypothesis indicated that glossolalists do feel better about themselves after speaking in tongues. This subjectively reported feeling of well-being is greater than for the control group which does not speak in tongues.

Hypothesis 4 was not supported. When interviewed and tested a year later, it was found that the tongue-speakers' sense of well-being persisted.

INTERPRETATION AND DISCUSSION OF THESE RESULTS—FIRST HYPOTHESIS

The Thematic Apperception Test (TAT) was used to check our prediction that glossolalists were less independent in the presence of an authority figure than were non-tongue-speakers.[3]

The TAT is made up of some twenty pictures. The subject is asked to make up a story about what is happening in the pictures, which actually are quite vague. A person can read almost anything he wishes into the pictures. In this way he reveals a great deal about himself.

We particularly wanted to find out if the subject was inner-

---

3. The original statistical operation called for the "t" test based on the differences between 20 pairs—each composed of a tongue speaker and a non-tongue-speaker. We encountered an interesting difficulty with seven of our non-tongue-speakers; although six of them were indeed nonglossolalists when tested we discovered in the course of our study that they had at one time spoken at least a phrase or two in tongues. A seventh person had actually been a regularly practicing glossolalist, and then gave up the practice. We felt that it was necessary to eliminate all seven from Group B.

This required a change in the statistical procedure. The formula for determining the differences between the means of two small uncorrelated samples was used. Inasmuch as six additional tongue-speakers had originally been interviewed and tested, it was decided to use all 26 subjects as members of Group A. The statistical differences were thus finally determined from a group of 26 glossolalists, and 13 nonglossolalists. The number of non-tongue-speakers then appeared to be small for purposes of scientific research. However, we were in effect comparing tongue-speakers with a control group of many hundreds of religious persons whom we have tested and interviewed during the past fifteen years. In the course of the author's practice as a psychologist and psychoanalyst, he has tested more than 500 seminarians and clergymen, and conducted intensive psychotherapy with approximately 175 clergy, plus a larger, uncounted number of religiously active laymen. Further, he has conducted psychotherapy with twelve active tongue-speakers. While the information from these sources is not statistically included in this research, the wealth of data gained from these contacts provided a background for comparing tongue-speakers and non-tongue-speakers.

directed, able to see himself as an individual, responsible for himself, or whether he was dependent in his behavior and easily directed by others. An example of a story that discloses a high degree of autonomy follows: "Though her parents are angry and forewarn of dire consequences, and friends mock her, she is firm in her decision, and will carry it out." Weak autonomy is evidenced by this story: "She hasn't the strength to go to the doctor alone, and will see if her husband will come home from the office, or if her mother will meet her there."

The results of our tests showed that the autonomy ratings of the nonglossolalists were significantly higher than those of the glossolalists. The glossolalist typically relied on paternalistic or maternalistic figures to produce the conclusions of their TAT stories.

The independence of the nonglossolalist is exemplified in this story: "I see age and youth here . . . trying to put over her will on the younger person. The younger is looking to the future. No two people can live the same life. She has to decide for herself."

A glossolalist characteristically told stories in which the conclusion was worked out by someone other than the figure with whom he identified himself and who dominated him. For instance, a thirty-two-year-old, married, male tongue-speaker told the following six stories. The numbering and lettering are the ones used to identify the actual TAT pictures.

Picture No. 4: (A man and woman talking together) "It looks like that woman is trying to get her husband to do something and he doesn't want to do it. She might love him quite a bit. It turns out pretty good. They both love each other. She talked him into doing whatever she wanted him to do."

Picture No. 6 BM: (An older woman and younger man standing together) "This is a mother and a son who did something that made her pretty angry or worried. The boy is ashamed of what he did. He probably gets a good scolding."

Picture No. 7 BM: (An older man and younger man in discussion) "The old man is trying to give the young man some advice—on the way to doing things in life. It looks like he's getting some pretty good advice. The way the young man is listening, he's taking the advice of the old man."

Picture No. 12 M: (A boy on a bed with an older man at his bedside) "It looks like the boy is sick. The old man is kneeling and praying. He's ready to lay hands on him. The boy gets to be all right."

Picture No. 13 MF: (A partly naked woman in bed, a man standing) "The guy is married. In bed with this woman, and feels pretty ashamed of himself. He confessed all his sins when he got home."

Picture No. 18 BM: (A man being clutched from behind) "Somebody's got ahold of this guy. He did something wrong. It could be the cops that have him. He's trying to run away from something. He probably got punished for whatever he did."

The "other person" always decided the outcome of these episodes. The main character was always subordinated. While the storyteller was thirty-two years old, age and authority dominated in every case. He was outer-directed. The TAT reveals in a striking manner individual differences in life-style. Our glossolalists told stories in which someone else solved the problem. Our nonglossolalists told stories in which the main character solved his own problems.[4]

---

4. The McKenzie Mental Health Scale designed for use with the TAT was employed for rating a subject's autonomy. It is a 5-point rating scale. All the TAT stories of the subjects were rated "blind" by two psychologists, independently of each other. The correlation was above .75. On the McKenzie TAT rating scale for autonomy, a rating of "one" indicates little autonomy. The tongue-speakers received a mean rating of 2.08 and the non-tongue-speakers a mean autonomy of 3.15—which indicates a statistica'ly significant difference between the two groups. The difference is significant at better than the 5% level of confidence, two-tailed test of significance. The finding is that tongue-speakers are more dependent on authority figures than are the non-glossolalists; dependency is here defined as being other-directed.

SECOND HYPOTHESIS

Our interviews with the tongue-speakers had already indicated how essential it was for a potential tongue-speaker to have a close relationship with the leader who was helping him. A complete sense of trust and confidence in the leader is vital. The following phrases were used to describe various leaders of the tongue-speaking groups: "That man is a holy man." "He is fantastic, I never met someone who is as sincere and dedicated as he is." "He truly lives every moment close to the Lord." "She is utterly charismatic, her whole life is a gift from God to the rest of us."

It was often difficult to distinguish whether glossolalists were talking about their leader or about Jesus. The leaders were regarded with a special quality of adoration, in such a way that it was difficult for an observer to know where the influence of the leader stopped and that of Jesus began. An intimate, prayerful address was used in approaching both Jesus and the tongue-leaders.

When Mrs. Rogers, with whose story we began this book, spoke in tongues at the kitchen sink, she did so with a sense of need, and she focused her thoughts and feelings on her sense of belonging to Jesus, and to her sense of closeness to her tongue-speaking group, and particularly on the very comfortable feeling of being accepted by her friend, Irene, who was the leader of the charismatic movement in her church.

When our glossolalists spoke in tongues, they always maintained positive feelings for their group leader. In fact, it appeared absolutely necessary that they have a relationship of continuing trust and confidence if they were to experience glossolalia as spiritually important and meaningful.

It is not surprising that a profound sense of trust in a leader is necessary for beginning to speak in tongues, just as it is for the induction of hypnosis. But a persisting relationship of trust appears to be equally vital if the practice is to continue to be an important part of one's life.

THIRD AND FOURTH HYPOTHESES

By means of these hypotheses we intended to compare feelings of depression experienced by tongue-speakers and non-tongue-speakers; and we wanted to compare the tongue-speakers with themselves after an interval of a year, to see if their feelings had changed.

The Minnesota Multiphasic Personality Inventory (MMPI) was used for this segment of our research. The MMPI is said to be the most widely used personality test in the world. There are approximately 500 true-false questions, the answers to which are profiled to indicate a dozen important indicators of emotional functioning.

The results of this test revealed that glossolalists were characteristically less depressed than nonglossolalists. When tested a year later, the glossolalists continued to experience the same feelings of well-being; they were no more—nor less—depressed than a year previously.[5] They continued to say that they were "changed persons" and continued to feel a definite assurance

5. The mean Depression score of the glossolalists on the MMPI was 46.7, and for the nonglossolalists it was 54.1. This difference is significant at the .01 level, two-tailed test of significance. When retested a year later, the glossolalists again had a mean Depression score of 46. There were no other significant changes on the overall MMPI profiles, either between the two groups, or after a year's interval for the tongue-speakers. The finding is that the feelings of well-being reported by the glossolalists apparently are maintained, at least after one years' continued use of this practice.

It should be noted, of course, that neither group would be considered to be clinically depressed. The normal person, on the average, would obtain a mean score of 50 on the Depression scale of the MMPI, and any score between 40 and 60 is thought by psychologists to be a "healthy" score. Therefore, the glossolalists mean score of 46.7 and the nonglossolalists mean score of 54.1 are both well within the normal range. Nonetheless, the difference between the mean scores is statistically significant; the glossolalists are clearly less depressed than the nonglossolalists.

that God loved them. Furthermore, they described themselves as more sensitive and loving toward others. Many felt they had better marital, including sexual, relationships. Most reported higher moral and ethical responsiveness, which they attributed to the glossolalia experience.

Tongue-speakers have had a profound experience of feeling that they are well; for most of them it has been a physical, emotional, and intellectual experience. Tongue-speaking gave them a physical sensation that they had never had before—their tongues did things that seemed impossible. Emotionally, the experience was one of fantastic release, comparable in intensity to sexual orgasm, or to the sense of freedom just after an intense stomach cramp subsides. And intellectually the impact was not unlike that experienced on being told by your favorite professor of an $A+$ on a final, comprehensive examination.

It is easy to see why tongue-speakers are less depressed than non-tongue-speakers. Depression is a feeling that the cupboard of the world is bare, that good things are not possible for one-self, and that the supply of good things in the world "out there" is terribly limited. A glossolalist believes that God Almighty, Creator of the ends of the universe, is with him and approves of him, and that helping fellow believers surround him and con-firm him in his belief that he is all right. It is hard to conceive of a more powerful antidote to feeling depressed.

Feeling supremely confident because of his experience of divine approval, the glossolalist is willing to risk more in life, to be bolder in his work, even to be more active in bed with his wife! Confident that his cupboard will be full again tomorrow, he can afford to be generous today. Whereas depression is characterized by the feeling of inner emptiness, the glossolalist is "filled" by the Spirit. Should he feel a bit down, he can begin to speak in tongues and recall that God is with him, that glosso-lalia is a special gift from God, and that he can unload his problems through releasing his feelings in tongue-speech. Each time he speaks in tongues, he performs a physical act which he surrounds with a set of beliefs reconfirming that he is a special person, specially blessed.

FIFTH HYPOTHESIS

Linguistic scholars work with precise definitions of what constitutes a natural human language. Glossolalia fails to meet the criteria of these definitions. Specifically, the work by Charles F. Hockett (in Joseph H. Greenberg, ed., *Universals of Language,* 1963) details sixteen criteria for language. The research of linguists clearly reveals that the spoken utterances of glossolalists do not meet these criteria.[6]

6. A more technical explanation of the linguistics of glossolalia lies outside the scope of this volume. For a careful account of why glossic utterances cannot be human languages, see Dr. Eugene A. Nida's *Glossolalia: A Case of Pseudo-Linguistic Structure.* The works by Dr. William J. Samarin, especially "The Linguisticality of Glossolalia," are helpful in explaining the differences between glossolalia and natural human languages.

6

Essential Differences: *Are Glossolalists Mentally Healthier than Others or Less So?*

OVERALL MENTAL HEALTH

Perhaps the most significant finding of this research is that one group is not any more mentally healthy than the other. On any broad criteria of emotional well-being, the tongue-speakers and non-tongue-speakers were about the same.

What does it mean when we say that the two groups were equally healthy mentally? Here were our criteria: mental health is the ability to receive and give love and to take responsibility—to be loving and to do productive work. There are people who believe in God, who wear long hair, who believe Christ provides for their material needs, and who are mentally healthy. There are also people with those same three qualities who are not mentally healthy—that is, they are not loving and responsible in their behavior toward themselves and others.

Our conclusion was that tongue-speakers and non-tongue-speakers proved equivalent in their ability to be loving and to do responsible work. The psychological test data and the personal interviews provided the evidence for this conclusion.

PERSONALITY TYPES

The next major finding concerned whether the tongue-speakers were of a special personality type. Did they tend to be hysterical or compulsive, or manic, or any other particular diagnostic category? Our study answered an unequivocal No. The glossolalists represented a cross section of all the usual personality types; they employed the full range of personality mechanisms and character defenses. This came to us as a surprise. Nevertheless, the finding that tongue-speakers were spread across the broad spectrum of mental illness and health, across the broad ranges of socioeconomic status and also of intelligence and education, was corroborated again and again.

Seven major character patterns were found among tongue-speakers and among non-tongue-speakers. (1) Exaggerated dependency reactions, marked by insatiable demands on others for almost every conceivable sort of gratification. (2) Submissive techniques, evident in a life-style of ingratiation, compliance, passivity, humility, and obedience. (3) Expiatory techniques, consisting of self-criticism and self-punishment, in order to avoid criticism and punishment from others. (4) Dominating techniques, which coerce people to yield to the individual's will. (5) Techniques of aggression, in which both subtle and direct forms of violence against the environment are used to gratify the individual's emotional needs. (6) Techniques of withdrawal, in which the individual protects his feelings by avoiding the possibility of competition, or rejection, or failure, or of feeling inferior. (7) Techniques aimed at the expansion of self-image, characterized by desire for constant admiration, for flattery, and for appreciation.[1]

1. A more complete description of these character drives appears in L. R. Wolberg and J. P. Kildahl, *The Dynamics of Personality* (New York: Grune & Stratton, 1970), pp. 120-129.

There were significant differences between the two groups, but they involved subtle personality variables rather than major differences of mental health or personality types. It was necessary to employ more sophisticated psychological and psychiatric methods to isolate these variables.

THE DEPENDENCY SYNDROME

The principal difference between tongue-speakers and non-tongue-speakers was that the glossolalists developed deeply trusting and submissive relationships to the authority figures who introduced them to the practice of glossolalia. Without complete submission to the leader, speaking in tongues was not initiated. In psychotherapy, this is called dependent transference. We noted repeatedly that persons who did not speak in tongues had a different relationship to authority figures than did the tongue-speakers.

There were no loners among the tongue-speakers. They banded together and were mutually supporting. We never met a deeply involved tongue-speaker who did not have some leader to whom he looked for guidance. Even in casual questioning about their glossolalia experiences, tongue-speakers very quickly mentioned the name of the person whom they revered as their model for tongue-speaking.

RELIANCE ON EXTERNAL AUTHORITY

Our tongue-speakers had a strong need for external guidance from some trusted authority. That is, they had a strong sense of leaning on someone more powerful than themselves, who gave them security and direction in their lives. To have such an authority figure often brought great peace and relaxation.

Often it appeared that tongue-speakers overinvested their

feelings in their leaders, idealizing them as nearly perfect parents. The adulation accorded the leader was the most obvious characteristic of tongue-speaking groups. At no time was this degree of reverence for a leader observed in non-tongue-speaking groups.

One glossolalist, a prominent businessman, always brought his pastor-leader along for on-site inspection of any new venture he was considering. A woman leader we interviewed received a couple of dozen phone calls per day from her group. "Just checking in," was the way that they described the purpose of the calls. The extraordinary number of hours glossolalists spent with one another, most importantly in the presence of the leader, was significant.

THE PRESSURE OF THE LEADER

It was not the speaking in tongues that brought the great feelings of euphoria that these people do experience. Rather it was the submission to the authority of the leader and to the sense of acceptance that followed this submission. The follower felt at peace because he had abandoned himself to the control of somebody else in the major and ultimate issues of his mental and emotional and spiritual experience.

A little girl walking down the street holding her daddy's hand feels serene and safe in a unique way. She holds his big, strong hand, and she rests joyfully in the belief that nothing can happen that her daddy cannot handle. She feels loved, and she feels protected.

Our research gave evidence that the believing tongue-speaker approaches this same feeling of euphoria. He believes that he is in the hands of God. He believes that he has proof of it, because he can speak in tongues.

Once having acquired the ability to speak in tongues, a person did not lose the facility for making such fluent, unintelligible sounds. But he could and often did lose the feeling of well-being that came upon him when he first spoke in tongues.

The drop in euphoria occurred when the tongue-speaker ceased to feel good about the experience itself, when he no longer fully trusted the leader who first taught him how to speak in tongues; sometimes this was because the sense of acceptance from the leader was missing. At other times it was because the follower no longer looked at his leader with admiration.

Here is an illustration of why one loses the feelings of well-being. Suppose that you were a young psychoanalyst who had been befriended by Sigmund Freud himself, who told you that he had seen in you extraordinary gifts of intelligence, insight, and an astounding ability to do psychoanalysis. You would feel ten feet tall, because Sigmund Freud was like a god to you, and now you had his personal stamp of approval. Then as time went on, you began to see flaws in Freud's system of psychoanalysis, and indeed you began to see personal flaws in Freud himself. His system did not work in every instance; Freud tended to be doctrinaire and adamant that there was only one right way to do psychoanalysis. He seemed to become bitter in the face of criticism, and he was downright jealous when others received some of the glory. Now when Freud gave you a compliment, it did not mean as much to you. If he said to you that you were a brilliant exponent of his method, it did not do much for you, because you realized that there were other important methods for treating emotional disorders. Sure, you still knew how to do psychoanalysis, but it did not have that same ring of authenticity for you that it once had.

One woman tongue-speaker lost her enthusiasm for the experience because she thought her pastor was overemphasizing it. She said, "He seems to have it as his one and only hobby. He must write a hundred letters a month to other tongue-speakers around the world. It seems to me that he is pushing it every chance he gets. He seems driven to impress people with it. It doesn't seem right."

In our interviews with persons who had formerly spoken in tongues and were now indifferent to the experience, the common cause in each case was a falling out with the leader of the tongue-speaking group. Consequently, each was deprived of his feeling of acceptance and contentment and well-being.

The importance of the leader was well illustrated by the fact that the style of glossolalia adapted by the group bore a close resemblance to the way in which the leader spoke. A linguist engaged in glossolalia research found that prominent visiting speakers affected whole groups of glossolalists. Although no two tongue-speakers sounded exactly alike, if the prominent leader spoke in a kind of Old Testament Hebraic style, those who were taught by him also spoke in this manner. If the leader of the group evidenced Spanish diction and mannerisms, his followers also developed that style. It is not uncommon for linguists to be able to tell which prominent itinerant glossolalist has introduced a congregation to tongue-speaking. Relatively few men and women travel the tongue-speaking circuit. The glossolalic styles of Bennett, Bredesen, Christenson, du Plessis, Mjorud, and Stone are distinctive enough to be identifiable by observant linguists.

REGRESSION

The deep subordination to an authority figure required for learning to speak in tongues involves a type of speech regression. The ego is partially abandoned; that is, the ego ceases its conscious direction of speech. Subordination also involves emotional regression; without it there cannot be the unconscious, automatic, and fluent selection of audible syllables which constitutes glossolalia.

HYPNOTIZABILITY

The ability to submit oneself to a mentor is a personality variable that cuts across all the usual personality types. It is not a correlate of either mental health or mental illness. Rather, this capacity exhibits the same general traits as does hypnotizability. The hypnotizable person can be described as one who has rich subjective experiences in which he can become deeply involved; one who reaches out for new experiences and is thus friendly to hypnosis; one who is interested in the life of the mind, not simply a competitive activist; and one who accepts impulses from within and is not afraid to relinquish reality testing for a time.

Hilgard states that "it is easy to see how many of the characteristics that we have enumerated . . . are part and parcel of childhood: the blurring of fantasy and reality, the involvement in 'pretend games,' the implicit following of adult words, the enjoyment of sensation, the feelings of excitement and of omnipotence. They form an attractive arena for the interpretation of regressive phenomena."[2]

Hypnotizability is not something that can be characterized as good or bad, as healthy or unhealthy. It is a trait found everywhere. At the same time, the inability to be hypnotized is also ubiquitous. Hypnotizability requires that the subject be trusting enough to turn himself fully over to someone else and place his destiny in his hand. Some people are not able to develop that kind of a trusting relationship and consequently cannot be hypnotized. Yet some individuals who cannot at first be hypnotized can develop that ability if their trust toward a leader increases.

It is our thesis that hypnotizability constitutes the *sine qua non* of the glossolalia experience. If one can be hypnotized, then one is able under proper conditions to learn to speak in tongues.

2. E. Hilgard, *Hypnotic Susceptibility* (New York: Harcourt, Brace & World, 1965), p. 342.

While glossolalia is not the same as hypnosis, it is similar to it and has the same roots in the relationship of the subject to the authority figure.

Let us suppose that a person has been hypnotized by a benevolent figure and is given posthypnotic suggestions that he will feel better, stronger, more relaxed, and more able to take life in stride. The hypnotized person will usually begin to experience some of these subjective changes in his mood. In like manner, the person who is induced to speak in tongues is told that the practice carries with it a variety of benefits, that it is a sign of God's approval, and that the speaker has been singled out for a special blessing. Therefore, as with hypnosis, tongue-speaking brings with it a postexperience suggestion of a sense of well-being. Similarly, what one expects to feel from smoking marijuana will also influence how the marijuana affects him.

Whenever one strives to reach a goal, and the goal is expected to produce a variety of benefits, a feeling of elation will accompany the reaching of it. Perseverance of the elation depends on whether or not the experience is reinforced by one's fellow practitioners, and whether or not persons continue to help each other to believe that this experience is indeed a mark of being blessed. Weight Watchers, Inc., for instance, uses the reinforcement principle very effectively. So do tongue-speakers. They join a group of their fellow practitioners, and they support each other in multiple ways so that they feel themselves to be a company of special people.

Our study has produced conclusive evidence that the benefits reported by tongue-speakers which are subjectively real and continuous are dependent upon acceptance by the leader and other members of the group rather than upon the actual experience of saying the sounds. Whenever a tongue-speaker broke off the relationship with the leader or the group, or felt rejected by the group, the experience of glossolalia was no longer so subjectively meaningful.

The solitary tongue-speaker—that is, one not surrounded by a company of fellow believers and practitioners—derived relatively less psychological benefit from the experience. While he may have felt specially singled out, he needed the constant reinforcement and encouragement of his fellow practitioners if he were to experience the subjective gains he first felt when he began to speak in tongues and was welcomed into a select fellowship.

The tongue-speaker who moved away from his home base lost something of the safety and stimulation that initially sustained him. If he found himself in a community where there was no tongue-speaking, he got much less of an emotional lift from his practice. For a short period the memory of the acceptance of his former group, and especially of his former leader, helped him to value his speaking in tongues. But without regular buoying up from others, the frequency and the meaning of his glossolalia experience diminished.

Solitary tongue-speakers do not often make themselves known. We encountered very few in the course of our research. None showed the exuberance that was characteristic of tongue-speakers who practiced in groups.

The solitary tongue-speaker would ask, "Well, what are you learning about glossolalia?"

The group member said, "Come join us. Would you like to receive the gift of the Holy Spirit?"

7

Psychological Factors in the Glossolalia Experience

Significant differences between tongue-speakers and non-tongue-speakers emerge when the two groups are investigated in depth. Certain specific psychological characteristics appear to be an integral part of the glossolalia experience.

ANXIETY OVER A LIFE CRISIS

Dr. Paul Qualben learned through careful interviewing that more than 85% of the tongue-speakers had experienced a clearly defined anxiety crisis preceding their speaking in tongues. Their anxiety was caused by marital difficulties, financial concerns, ill health, and general depression. Sometimes the crisis was of an ethical or religious nature and involved concern about spiritual values, guilt, and the ultimate meaning and purpose of life.

One man found himself having the urge to hug and kiss the men in his office with whom he worked. This shook him up so profoundly that he sought counseling from a clergyman, who happened to be a glossolalist. Ten days later he was speaking in tongues.

Another was hesitant about accepting a job promotion. He

was a junior executive and had been asked to become a vice-president of the moderate-sized company where he worked. The position involved being a hatchet man for the company—putting pressure on inefficient agencies, firing the losers, and being the front man for the president when a controversial issue had to be discussed. It also meant a lot of travel. The prospect frightened him, but he wanted the challenge. During his period of indecision, he began to speak in tongues. Then, he accepted the vice-presidency.

A woman subject began to speak in tongues within a week after her husband finally joined Alcoholics Anonymous. His drinking had been out of control for months, and they had been having many ugly moments together. Finally he consented, after a binge that had lasted a week, to go to an AA meeting. Six days later, at the Wednesday night meeting of her suburban Episcopal church, she began to pray in tongues. About a month later her husband also spoke in tongues.

Preoccupation with internal psychological factors seemed to create the necessary atmosphere in which a person was ready to speak in tongues and subsequently found some kind of answer to his problem. Loneliness and a sense of worthlessness or purposelessness made the glossolalia experience an appealing answer to self-doubt. Anxiety-free individuals were less apt to seek this kind of experience, to find it necessary or understandable.

In the control group—that is, among those who did not speak in tongues—interviews revealed that only approximately 30% of the subjects had experienced similar anxiety crises, as opposed to 85% for the tongue-speaking group. The difference is statistically significant, and we believe anxiety is a prerequisite for developing the ability to speak in tongues.

In addition, it should be noted that the very experience of learning to speak in tongues generated anxiety. Those who attended meetings where glossolalia was discussed were generally under group pressure to "do the right thing." That is, demonstrate their approbation of the venture by speaking in tongues.

The uncertainty about what was going to happen, the eerie feeling that "maybe it will happen to me" or "it should happen to me" combined to produce nervous tension that was a crisis situation in itself.

REGRESSION

Psychological regression was another emotional factor shown to be inherent in the development of the glossolalia experience. By regression is meant a reversion to an earlier level of maturity, during which the rational, common-sense, ego-controlled way of relating to life is somehow diminished. It is perhaps more childlike, less critical, and generally more free-floating in its nature. The glossolalia experience was generally introduced under the mass pressures of a group or a crowd, or the atmosphere was contagious because of the leader's charisma. The neophytes' critical faculties were subdued.

Without exposure to a regressive group experience, glossolalia could not be induced. The glossolalia experience was rarely generated in the course of quiet, rational introspection.

THE MATURITY OF THE PERSON

As with many other experiences, the use to which glossolalia is put is often a reflection of emotional maturity. In our study persons with a low level of emotional stability tended to be extreme in their affirmation of the benefits of glossolalia. A well-integrated tongue-speaker generally made no wildly exaggerated claims for its powers, used it in a way that was not sensational, and did not allow it to dominate his life or use it as an instrument by which to manipulate others. In marked contrast, glossolalists who reported speaking in tongues at every moment they were not speaking English were psychologically in a similar condition to those who have an obsessive fantasy regarding numbers, or a hand-washing compulsion. Some claimed unusual gifts, including healing, prophecy, special wisdom, interpretation of world events, and discernment of mysterious phenomena. Often they were not amenable to reasonable discussion with other people.

A seminarian we interviewed was sure that he could "blow their minds" the first time he spoke in tongues during chapel exercises. He planned the performance carefully in advance, choosing just the right moment for the maximum effect. He succeeded only in making a spectacle of himself and alienating the rest of the student body.

Nevertheless, some glossolalists used their ability in private devotional experiences and found it to be uplifting. They reported that they were much helped by it and felt they could use it in a controlled manner.

One tongue-speaker prayed inaudibly in tongues as he made his way from the Communion rail back to his pew following the sacrament of the Lord's Supper. He felt it an ineffably spiritual experience, and through it he was able to give vent to his inner life even though the sounds he made were beyond his comprehension. He made no demands for the attention of others, he merely "did his own thing."

It appeared to us at the conclusion of our research that the more integrated the personality, the more modest he was in both claims and practice of glossolalia. Those who stated that they solved virtually every problem with which they wrestled by means of glossolalia were generally fundamentally immature.

THE MAGICAL QUALITY

All tongue-speakers entertained a certain magical notion of what glossolalia meant. The term magical was defined by the belief that God or the Holy Spirit controlled and directed believers' lives in a *mechanistic* way. For instance, one person in the glossolalia group prayed, "God, make me a puppet." He believed almost literally that God would pull the strings and he as a puppet would respond. Others declared, "God now directs my life; that is, God directly controls the movement of my tongue; and He allows me to make these sounds." Such believers usually developed tremendous feelings of worth and power. "To think that God has singled me out to make that very sound!" was a typical self-assessment.

One woman told us that when she could not find her scissors, she would pray in tongues, close her eyes while standing in the middle of a room, and turn around rapidly several times until she felt like stopping. Whatever way that she faced when she stopped was the direction in which the Lord wanted her to walk in order to find her scissors. When asked if this method ever failed, she replied that if she did not find the scissors in the direction she walked, it meant that "the Lord was telling me to do something else where he did direct me."

THE PLACE OF THE IRRATIONAL

In our survey the irrational was tied closely to the magical quality with which many glossolalists invested their experience. Their glossolalia was irrational in the sense that the speakers did not attempt to conceptualize or understand it within the framework of their usual world; in fact, they asserted that it could not be validated by other persons, especially by somebody who did not enter into the system. They said the experience was impossible to confirm scientifically because it was a private matter; its claims could not be proven or disproven.

Hartmann discussed a parallel to this kind of speech in his writings on deautomatization. A person acts in a deautomatized manner when he overflows with emotions that are so overpowering that he speaks in nonconscious language. It happens on those occasions when all the emotions experienced simply cannot be verbalized, and out pour sounds which are relatively unintelligible. The tongue-speaker's act is similar except that he believes that it is directed by the Holy Spirit. Whereas a nonreligious person might simply say he is overflowing with feeling and emotions, the tongue-speaker also believes that God is making his tongue move, even that God is actually speaking through him.

Some tongue-speakers were irritated by our investigation. One handed us a written statement—so that we could not mistake his meaning—saying, "You think you can psychoanalyze the gift of the Holy Spirit even if it is of divine origin. It seems presumptuous to think that science can probe and analyze such divine manifestations. Personally, I think this is hallowed ground and lies outside the realm of scientific analysis. If you try to analyze it, you will surely fail. A person who does not speak in tongues can no more explain what glossolalia means than an unconverted person can analyze what takes place in a true conversion to Christ."

INTERPRETATION OF TONGUES

The interpretation of glossolalia is regarded as a special ability, in fact, a spiritual gift of value equivalent to tongue-speaking itself (I Cor. 12:10). Only a few persons report having this ability, and it is relatively rare that a person is able both to speak in tongues and to interpret what his own and others' tongue-speaking means.

We attended many meetings where glossolalia both occurred and was interpreted, and noted that the interpretations were usually of a very general nature. After a segment of tongue-speech, an interpreter commonly offered the explanation that the speaker had been thanking and praising God for many blessings. Another frequent theme was that the speaker was asking for strength and guidance for himself and for others.

However, perhaps a third of the time, the interpreter offered specific interpretations of what glossolalists said. More rarely, an interpreter "translated" phrase by phrase and sentence by sentence. In order to investigate the accuracy of these interpretations, we undertook to play a taped example of tongue-speech privately for several different interpreters of tongues. In no instance was there any similarity in the several interpretations. The following typifies our results: one interpreter said the tongue-speaker was praying for the health of his children; another that the same tongue-speech was an expression of gratitude to God for a recently successful church fund-raising effort.

When confronted with the disparity between their interpretations, the interpreters offered the explanation that God gave to one person one interpretation of the speech and to another person another interpretation. They showed no defensiveness about being cross-examined and generously upheld alternative interpretations as equally valid. The interpreters offered their remarks with sincerity and good faith; there was no evidence of conscious scheming or manipulation.

We know of a man who was raised in Africa, the son of missionary parents, who decided—rather cynically perhaps—to test the interpretation of tongues. He attended a tongue-speaking meeting where he was a complete stranger. At the appropriate moment, he rose and spoke the Lord's Prayer in the African dialect he had learned in his youth. When he sat down, an interpreter of tongues at once offered the meaning of what he had said. He interpreted it as a message about the imminent second coming of Christ.

FEELINGS OF WORTHLESSNESS

An experience invariably concomitant with the onset of speaking in tongues and described by every tongue-speaker interviewed, usually in the same way, was a sense of worthlessness. This feeling had many of the marks typical of depression, but it generally also had a personal reference. Glossolalists reported that they felt they had nothing in themselves that was valuable or worthwhile, that they were empty, heavy, and powerless. One of them said, "I felt like a little child who could only say 'Goo.' "

These feelings were not the same as guilt feelings. They were usually not attached to any specific act or deeds. They did not refer to a particular condition which made them feel worthless. There was simply a total sense of nothingness and worthlessness.

Initiate tongue-speakers told us that religious services had further intensified their feelings of worthlessness, specifically because they made them feel inferior for not yet having spoken in tongues, when many of the congregation could already do so. Their feeling of worthlessness lifted and was replaced by a tremendous euphoria as soon as they learned to speak in tongues. Glossolalia was seen as dramatic evidence of a changed spiritual condition. It was considered a tangible indication that one was indeed a different person—an outward and visible sign of receipt of a spiritual gift. As is typical in many conversion experiences, the neophyte changes some material thing about himself—his dress, or his habits, or friends; in this case it was his speech.

JUNG'S THEORY

Because the glossolalic act does not begin as the result of simple, conscious choice—say, as one decides to brush his teeth and then does it—the subject has the feeling that outside forces are responsible for the experience. One speaker said, "I tried and tried to speak in tongues and I couldn't do it. Then late one night long after the meeting was over, I found myself suddenly speaking in tongues." Another tongue-speaker dreamed first that he was speaking in tongues. And then when he awoke, he found that he could speak in tongues.

The successful glossolalist felt that an outside cause lent external validation to his tongue-speech and to himself as a total person. According to Carl Jung, this meets the criteria for a genuine religious experience, because it involves an experience of the numinous, which seizes and controls the subject, who is acted upon by it rather than being its creator. The neophyte tongue-speaker casts aside his intense feelings of worthlessness and sees himself specially marked by divine approval.

In contrast, I prefer to define a religious experience by its fruits, rather than by how it is induced. Excellent and sufficient behavioral criteria for religion are offered by the Old Testament prophet Micah: to do justice, to love kindness, and to walk humbly with God. In the New Testament, the letter of James urges that true religion consists of helping those in need. To accept Jung's criteria, which terms religious any experience not brought about by the usual mechanisms of conscious choice, seems uncritical. For it fits any psychosis, all dreams, as well as the practice of glossolalia into the category of a religious experience.

SUMMARY

The consistency of the series of psychological manifestations preceding and accompanying the experience of glossolalia was marked. These conditions may, of course, appear apart from that particular experience. But it is our opinion that they occur virtually every time speaking in tongues is begun, and that they are prerequisites for it.

It may be well to state again in general that glossolalists are neither more nor less emotionally disturbed than equally religious non-tongue-speakers. Nevertheless, pronounced dependence on an authority figure regarded as benevolent, and prior need for acceptance by a group and by God, were characteristic of the tongue-speakers we interviewed. Once the ability had been achieved, a feeling of relaxation and euphoria followed, together with that of having found oneself and of having found a home in the company of other tongue-speakers. All the glossolalists we interrogated reported this to be the most exciting and thrilling experience of their lives.

8

Group Behavior and the Glossolalia Experience

Tongue-speakers band together, usually in highly visible groups. The following descriptions illustrate why these groups have experienced such intense difficulty in finding acceptance in mainline religious communities.

DIVISIVENESS

The presence of persons who speak in tongues, and of groups of tongue-speakers who psychologically band together, usually created a disturbance in the mainline Protestant congregations we studied. While there were examples of church groups which increased in numbers and strength as a result of the appearance of glossolalia, more usually friction and divisive factions developed.

In extreme examples, up to one-third of the congregation stopped going to church and/or dropped their formal membership. Usually, however, the loss was less. In most cases the leave-taking was not amicable or quiet. Usually there was bitterness, disappointment, and disruption when a congregation divided into those who espoused and those who opposed glossolalia.

Word passed rapidly as to who was the latest to "have the gift." And almost as quickly, an emotional barrier was thrown up between the new tongue-speaker and those who did not yet participate. Even brothers and sisters, or parents and children, became estranged. Communication was guarded. We interviewed one anxious father and mother whose college son had told them on the phone that he had begun to speak in tongues. They worried that he would be different. What would he think of them? Their meeting during Christmas vacation was strained as he tried to let his parents know that he was a "new person." It was several months before they were fully at ease together.

We noticed that church conventions often became occasions for tongue-speakers to seek each other out, to set up ad hoc sessions. The cabalistic nature of these meetings was perceived, often with bitterness, by nonglossolalic convention delegates.

Here are some quotations from members of glossolalia groups which convey their feeling of separation.

"We work the hardest in this church, we contribute the most generously, we constitute the majority of the Sunday-school teachers. None of us has stopped coming to church, or transferred our membership elsewhere. We love and support our pastor, who is an inspiring glossolalist. We don't want the others to leave. How can you say that we are the cause of the trouble?"

"People who don't speak in tongues are missing a most blessed experience. I can't understand their reluctance to seek this gift."

"We who speak in tongues only want to be loving to all members of the church. We cannot understand why we are singled out by them, and regarded with suspicion."

"It is so marvelous just to let go, and speak in words that only the Lord can give me. I wish everyone could have this gift."

"I resent that people are always trying to analyze what we are doing. We don't constantly analyze people who don't speak in tongues."

"There is nothing we do in any way that is divisive. We just want to be a blessing to the others."

"Our group has begun many marvelous works in the last four years, and I am sure we would never have done it if we had not had the gift of the Spirit. We were just not as dedicated before the Lord gave us his gift."

It should be noted that in these testimonies a feeling of defensiveness accompanies the feeling of being set apart. The tongue-speakers' tendency to overjustify and overrationalize their group's behavior is pronounced.

Generally, the charismatic movement has not made for easy compromise or impartiality; often it has polarized congregations. Since many of the churchgoers we interviewed thought of their institution as a private club, new opinion and new practice was looked upon with suspicion. Tongue-speaking often caused hard feelings. Because the tongue-speakers' experiences were so overwhelming, it was virtually unthinkable to treat them quietly; some sort of public announcement of what had taken place was needed. We found that the very great visibility of the movement caused battle lines to be quickly formed.

PROJECTION OF ANGER

Related to the divisiveness which speaking in tongues stimulates is the anger and frustration it generates within the tongue-speakers themselves. It was our finding that glossolalists handle these emotions in a way that is specific to them.

Anger of any kind does not disappear easily. It is not eradicated by intense emotional or religious experience. Rather, such experiences usually result only in its redirection. If, for example, after an emotional experience, a person becomes exceptionally loving, he may continue at the same time to be terribly angry with those who represent his former way of life. That is, he redirects his anger at them. We found that tongue-speakers we studied were generally very loving toward the members of their own groups. Their social concern extended to members of congregations like themselves and to people who potentially could become like them. However, they exhibited a subtle disrespect for non-tongue-speakers and toward those who showed no interest in joining their numbers.

Nonglossolalists were often made to feel inferior in the presence of a tongue-speaker, who usually managed to bring up somehow the subject of his attainments. Nonglossolalists usually anticipated this and gave some kind of defense as to why they were not involved or interested in participating. They were often asked if they wanted to seek the gift of tongues, and a simple No was rarely satisfactory. When we were conducting our research we raised many a quizzical and disappointed look when we told tongue-speakers that we were concerned only with *observing* glossolalia and not with trying to become tongue-speakers ourselves.

When one becomes a glossolalist one is at once provided with an in-group, while at the same time members of the out-group are defined. There is psychological security in this kind of polarization because one feels that he knows for sure where he stands, and it is easy to find an object for anger. One insists that it is the "other fellow" who harbors the ill will. The capacity for self-deception is, of course, always strong in us all, but it particularly flourishes in an atmosphere where there are two camps divided over a specific issue.

The problem of angry projection is classically illustrated by a Protestant missionary group in Latin America which divided sharply over glossolalia, split into two camps, and literally spent all their waking time in separate prayer meetings—each group praying for the other. The prayers were long and loud, and the shortcomings of the other group were repeatedly catalogued for the Lord, so that he would be sure exactly what was wrong with the members of the other group, how they were in error, and which of their qualities ought to be changed.

We noted that glossolalists, as a group, tended to employ this type of anger projection for handling their own anger.

"We have no authority figure in our group—except Jesus Christ. The passive pew-sitters in our various churches lean upon our kind to keep their educational programs and other church organizations alive." The manner of his explanation precisely demonstrated that, in fact, he was quite dependent on having an out-group—against which to vent his anger and which served to unite his group. There is nothing like having a common enemy to pull a group closer together.

GROUP CAMARADERIE

Generally, anger projection and group camaraderie are inter-related. It was evident to us that tongue groups become separate societies united by the phenomenon they experience together. They developed great intimacy among themselves. They were often outcasts from the broader society of the church because of their unusual behavior, but as a consequence held even more tightly together. As with any group which suffers persecution, they generally grew in cohesiveness.

The overall picture which presented itself to us was one in which tongue-speakers tended to be split off from the larger community of the church. By their behavior they indicated that they were most concerned for persons like themselves, despite their protestations that they were interested in the welfare of the entire church. If we evaluated their behavior rather than their words, it appeared that their anger had been redirected outward against groups who were unlike themselves. Despite their voiced concern that the whole church should be built up, they generally protested that they were innocent of any divisive qualities and that if the church at large would only accept them there would be harmony. The in-group feeling for each other was promoted as they provided solace for one another in the face of the criticism from the traditional church members. Of course, self-criticism was lacking on both sides. Nevertheless, the tongue-speakers created the division, inasmuch as they introduced the new practice. Their intense group camaraderie confirmed their own prejudices. The mechanism of anger projection was enhanced, imputing to other persons or groups the feelings of dislike which are denied in oneself. In voicing loving camaraderie for one another, glossolalists redirect some of their anger toward groups of fellow church members who are unlike themselves.

HISTRIONIC DISPLAY

Another group phenomenon which evidenced itself among glossolalists was a tendency toward histrionic display. It is true that the group usually took on the character of the leader. When the leader was exhibitionistic, so, too, were the followers. Where the leader tended to be quiet and reserved, the groups developed that quality of meeting. But even among staid Protestant congregations dramatic emotional displays occurred at glossolalia meetings. While we were conducting our study we witnessed tongue-speakers entranced by visions, exorcising demons, foretelling world events, and attempting bizarre methods of spiritual healing.

Yet they all believed that they were getting their words and powers from the Lord. The belief that tongue-speaking is caused by direct mechanical movement of the vocal chords by the Holy Spirit made group members accept almost anything that was uttered as glossolalia.

Dramatic displays are understandable, in terms of the structure of many glossolalia meetings. For example, they often began about eight o'clock in the evening with prayer and continued with testimonies, Bible study, and intermittent prayer until midnight. Only at that late hour might speaking in tongues begin. The length and intensity of the meeting produced a stressful situation which lowered the normal healthy, conscious resistance of the participants to excessive behavior. Because the situation was open-ended—that is, no one knew when it would finish—it generated a tension that called for closure. It became an anxiety-ridden, structureless occasion. One way an individual could structure it was to become a member, to join the others. Crowd psychology works on the individual in such an event.

The unstructured meeting and the resulting fatigue often combined with permissive leadership, provided the conditions under which an emotionally disturbed person could loosen his control and take part in histrionic displays that were neither psychologically integrating to the subject nor edifying to the group.

PREOCCUPATION WITH GLOSSOLALIA

A further characteristic of glossolalic group behavior was a preoccupation with their special endowment. It was very difficult for those who had undergone this experience not to give it a central place in life and spend time trying to understand it. Very few new tongue-speakers were able to be circumspect about their experience—rather they become salesmen for it. They were motivated to share it with others and hoped to teach other people to speak in tongues. Glossolalists have gone so far as to take hold of another person's chin saying, "Now you make the sound I've made and I'll move your chin," in order to help another speak in tongues. Often a nonglossolalist will spend hour upon hour with tongue-speakers who try by various methods to induce the experience.

One of our interviewees was up until 4 A.M. the night he learned to speak in tongues. The experience took place in the motel room of a friend on a Saturday night after a Georgia Tech football game. Each year the old fraternity brothers assembled for one game. Two of the men told about having learned to speak in tongues. Their enthusiasm for life, their success in business, and their feeling of being close to Christ made them the center of attention. Their mood was infectious. The Gideon Bible was brought out. First passages in Acts and I Corinthians were read, then our interviewee said he would like to hear what glossolalia sounded like. His friend quietly prayed in tongues. It sounded strange, but nothing more than that. It was one o'clock in the morning and most fellows were tired and so went back to their own rooms.

Our friend wanted to stay and hear more. He had learned a month earlier that his nine-year-old son had leukemia. That made him wonder if there really was a God—a God who affects what goes on in the world. He was searching. He wondered if life made any sense, and why lovely, innocent little children had to suffer. He wanted to talk about gut-level things: how he could bear the sorrow he knew would be his in the months and years ahead. Could he experience any assurance that there was some real love in the world?

As he remembered that night, the men who spoke in tongues really understood what he meant. One, an engineer, had lost his job because of the recession. He had been out of work eight months. Another had a mentally retarded child. He knew what it was to suffer. Both his friends knew what it was to need love and could talk about it freely with him.

They prayed together and read from the Bible and talked. They asked if he wanted to receive the gift of the Holy Spirit, and he said that he would try. One of the men asked him to imitate his words, "Anee, kitanee ashorum. O, anoramo anayano Jesu . . ." and then to kneel and pray.

One friend gently laid both his hands on top of his head. The other took the left and right side of his jaw in his thumb and first finger of each hand saying, "Now pray, Jim. Say what-

ever the Lord gives you to say, and I will move your mouth."
Abadaba abadaba rahbadaba ramanama . . . and the syllables
started to come smoothly. Tears flowed down his cheeks as
strange words issued from his mouth. He was speaking in
tongues.

It is our definite opinion that those who have the necessary
psychological characteristics can *learn* to speak in tongues. This
gives rise to the question, "If it is truly a gift of the Holy Spirit,
why must it be demonstrated and taught?"

SUMMARY

The author would like to offer a personal and subjective
summary of his reactions to the group behavior of tongue-
speakers.

I am skeptical of the sociological and psychological aspects of
tongue-speech as exhibited in public. Too much of it has been
harmful rather than helpful when measured by the criterion of
edifying the whole group. It is my belief that the glossolalia
experience should be evaluated by the criterion that has been
the traditional yardstick of the church: Does it "help to build
up the community," as St. Paul wrote in I Corinthians 14:5?

Tongue-speaking does not look very uniquely spiritual to me
after many experiences of watching people teach other people
how to speak in tongues. I have observed the same routine everywhere I have been: (1) a meeting devoted to intense concentra-
tion on tongue-speaking, followed by (2) an atmosphere of
heightened suggestibility to the words of the tongue-speaking
leader, after which (3) the initiate is able to make the sounds
he is instructed to make. It is the same procedure that a com-
petent hypnotist employs. Like the hypnotist, the tongue-speaking leader succeeds with some subjects and with others does not.
I have reached the conclusion that tongue-speaking is a learned
phenomenon.

I have the impression that the testimonies of the tongue-speakers are valid, honest statements of the way they feel. They do experience a subjective sense of well-being.

I was often irritated by tongue-speakers who reported that the sounds they were making had a divine, cosmic origin which linked the speakers to sources of omnipotent power. Such an explanation was offered to me immediately after I had seen tongue-speakers working hard at creating a semihypnotic emotional atmosphere in which some suggestible people had been able to learn to make these sounds.

The excesses of histrionic display and the occasional bizarre expressions of emotion and behavior might have been more tolerable to me if they had been accompanied by more self-criticism or curiosity about what they were doing. But the combination in this phenomenon of appearing to be a learned experience, attended by unusual behavior and rationalized by a spiritual explanation, produced in me a critical attitude toward glossolalia. Most of the scientific and religious community has had the same critical reaction to the public displays of speaking in tongues.

I appreciated the attitude of one tongue-speaker when he said, "I regret the unfortunate and exaggerated claims of those who are either for or against glossolalia and have consequently cut loose from their objectivity, and who seem to lack love for their brothers who differ with them." However, the following type of statement was heard more often: "I find your study upsetting. I feel that if you had more practical data concerning tongue-speaking, you would reach a different conclusion. Don't write us off. I'm offering you this challenge. Expose yourself fully to us, and then you will really know what the power of the Holy Spirit baptism is. I don't think that you believe that glossolalia is a gift of the Holy Spirit. And if that's so, even if you write a learned book on the subject, it would only bring more confusion."

9

Unanswered Questions

Having explored in depth the phenomena of glossolalia for several years, we are convinced that there is still much to be learned. We feel, in fact, that we have only grazed the surface.

FURTHER HYPNOTIC STUDIES

Since the present findings show that the ability to speak in tongues correlates with the ability to be hypnotized, we believe that empirical investigations should be undertaken to determine whether indeed all tongue-speakers can indeed be hypnotized. Ideally, one would gather individual tongue-speakers together and see if each could be hypnotized. But not all persons can be hypnotized by the same hypnotists, for a relationship of individual trust is crucial. We therefore propose that the Harvard Group Scale of Hypnotic Susceptibility, a screening device for group administration with self-reporting scoring, be used to grade large groups of glossolalists according to their apparent hypnotic susceptibility.

At the same time persons who have tried and failed to speak in tongues would also be graded, the assumption being that they may lack hypnotic susceptibility. Again, however, complications arise from the leader-follower relationship. Many therapists who use hypnosis in their medical and psychological practice find that sometimes, after a period of time, persons who have been unhypnotizable do develop the kind of trusting relationship which allows them to submit themselves to hypnosis.

A sympathetic non-tongue-speaker told us, "I personally feel that people like myself who are not gifted with tongue-speaking are being deprived of a very valuable experience. I would like to be blessed as they are. I wonder if you can see something in me psychologically that is blocking the Holy Spirit. And if you can see such a barrier, can you help me by psychological means to be more open to a spiritual gift?"

He posed a difficult question. He was a man who kept control of everything that he could, and had an ulcer to show for it. No secretary waited on him; he dialed his own phone calls and would have preferred to type his own letters. He drank milk every two hours and ate baby foods, a regression he could permit himself because of this ulcer. But he was the one who looked at his watch and told himself when to eat. He kept the jars of baby food in his own desk and opened them for himself. He would not, however, let himself regress by opening himself emotionally, so that he could be instructed by someone else how to speak in tongues.

It is possible, but improbable, that this man might slowly let his guard down sufficiently to establish a friendly and trusting relationship with some tongues teacher. Only then might he be able to learn to speak in tongues.

A fruitful related research procedure might be to ask tongue-speakers to speak in tongues while hypnotized. In view of the fact that they do not consciously know what they are saying, it might be enlightening to see if they could report the meaning of their utterances when they resumed a fully conscious state. Posthypnotic suggestions would be offered to the subjects to see what particular kinds of emotional memories and experiences they could recall.

Such corollary experiments as informing a person under hypnosis that he should later speak in tongues in a certain manner and say certain things with a particular meaning could also be conducted. The subject, not having been informed of the content of his posthypnotic suggestion, would speak in tongues, and observers would compare the posthypnotic suggestion with the behavior of the glossolalist.

LIFE CRISES AND THE ONSET OF GLOSSOLALIA

An ongoing survey of church groups in which there is pressure for members to speak in tongues would also prove of value. It might be worthwhile to see if a person in crisis tends to turn, in a more suggestible manner, to a spiritual leader who then helps him to initiate the practice of glossolalia. Our finding was that a personal crisis of some kind preceded the initial experience of speaking in tongues in 87% of the cases examined. We noted that where there was no crisis experience, there was less susceptibility toward learning to speak in tongues. Further, one glossolalist reported that as she became more settled in her life, her need to find solace and support from glossolalia was less urgent. It would seem that the use of glossolalia, with its special meaning of acceptance by God and by the group of fellow tongue-speakers, would diminish as a person solved his critical problems and became more independent. A study extending over a period of time needs to be made to determine whether continuing successful life adjustment tends to reduce tongue-speaking.

There are, of course, some "professional" tongue-speakers. These individuals travel throughout the world speaking and lecturing about the blessings of glossolalia. One is so well known that he boasts that he can come to a strange place and preach a sermon that does not refer to glossolalia or to the gifts of the Spirit, and still people will begin to speak in tongues following his sermon. It cannot be assumed that the persistence of their ability to speak in tongues is caused by continuing personal difficulties.

PERSONS WHO CEASE SPEAKING IN TONGUES

A more thorough investigation needs to be made of persons who once learned to speak in tongues, practiced it for some time, and then gave it up. In the course of our research for this book, seven erstwhile glossolalists were interviewed and tested, and it was found that the crucial factor for their stopping the practice was a falling out with the authority figure who had introduced them to it. We noted that while the ex-tongue-speaker could still speak in tongues if he tried, he reported that it did not seem to be a genuine experience with him and that he "did not feel any better for doing it." Psychologically speaking it did not provide the possibilities of positive transference or of regression that had previously made it an attractive means of personality adjustment.

A famous psychoanalyst was once seen by one of his patients eating lunch at a counter in an inexpensive New York cafeteria. The sight of his hero eating in such a place produced a profound feeling of mistrust and disappointment in the patient. "I wouldn't think of eating there," said the patient, "and if he is that kind of a person, what other mistakes in judgment might he make, including the way that he is proceeding to conduct my psychoanalysis." The patient's attitude was immature, to be sure, but he kept his doubts to himself and soon thereafter stopped treatment. The analyst's methods had not changed after the lunch in the cafeteria. His patient had idolized him up until that time. But after seeing him eat beans and franks, the magic went out of the analysis. This appears to be what happens when a tongue-speaker loses respect—whatever the reason—for his leader.

We are convinced that it is the transference relationship that brings the feelings of euphoria rather than the actual speaking in tongues. The unmistakable conclusion was that the saying of the glossolalia words and phrases brought little or no subjective sense of relief when those words were not embedded in the feeling and conviction that this was indeed a gift of God and highly esteemed by members of the glossolalia group. Those who ceased the practice of glossolalia were clearly ambivalent toward the leader. While they did not condemn all aspects of the experience, they indicated that they felt too much was made of it, that speakers spent too much time on it, that the leaders were not entirely sincere, and so forth.

Those who had spoken in tongues and then had given up the practice were no longer related in an intimate emotional way to any group of tongue-speakers. "They're not my type. I have different interests. We have just grown apart. We don't see eye to eye on speaking in tongues any more. I feel uncomfortable with them. It was taking up too much of my husband's and my time." These were some of the typical reasons offered by former group members for their lessening participation and declining interest.

One member resigned from a Pentecostal church because she felt oppressed by her minister's legalistic stand against smoking, drinking, dancing, and male-female relationships. She felt he limited her opportunities to marry. Some years later she was still vaguely troubled about her spiritual status and felt that perhaps she should return to the church. She could still speak fluently in tongues, but reported that it had no meaning for her because she was "out of fellowship with the Lord." It did not make her "feel good as it once did."

We noted that some tongue-speakers transferred their affections from the leader to other tongue-speakers. It was not uncommon for a clergyman to learn to speak in tongues from one leader, then as he moved about in the religious world to find a greater affinity for another leader. Such transference of affections involved no lessening of interest in or benefit from the glossolalia. However, we found no tongue-speaker who was unrelated to a glossolalia authority figure whom he esteemed.

When glossolalia was an important life goal there was always a relationship to a leader and/or to a group which conveyed a feeling of acceptance and belonging.

THE GROUP DYNAMICS OF THE MOVEMENT

Another investigation would probe sociological aspects of the movement. Studies to determine the vicissitudes of glossolalist groups might posit such questions as: What happens if the leader changes his emphasis? What is the natural length of life of a glossolalia group? What is its optimum size? The groups we studied were generally composed of twenty or thirty members.

NONRELIGIOUS GLOSSOLALIA

We noted in our historical survey that glossolalia is not a uniquely Christian or even a uniquely religious phenomenon. From a linguistic point of view, religiously inspired utterances have the same general characteristics as those that are not religiously inspired. Does the meaning of glossolalia vary from setting to setting? Does the experience differ when there are no religious dimensions involved?

Would it be possible to devise a totally different conceptual framework which would be equally successful in inducing the kind of speech which is now regarded as a "gift of the spirit?" Our finding was that the meaning of the event rather than the event itself is what confers psychological benefit on the speaker. What would the result be if a person were told that if he imitated an example of tongue-speech he would suffer harmful rather than beneficial consequences?

CHILDREN'S USE OF GLOSSOLALIA

While we know of children who speak in tongues, some as young as three or four years of age, we did not include their experience in our study. Do children learn to speak in a different fashion, or more or less readily than adults? Is the nature of their utterances simpler than that of an adult who has had a wider variety of verbal experiences? Does a child glossolalist have the same psychological sense of well-being as an adult tongue-speaker?

The ego psychologist Hartmann believes that it is threatening for a child to lose his ego control. It seems to us also that it would be dangerous to a child's sense of well-being to practice a form of speech which cuts him off from normal social contact and is described to him in "spiritual" terms. A little child feels the presence of enough things that are unreal—ghosts, monsters, and things that go bump in the night. He needs all the hold on reality that he can get.

NEUROLOGICAL QUESTIONS

A number of neurological questions also are raised by the phenomenon of glossolalia. Does a person regress neurologically as well as psychologically when he speaks in tongues? What part of the brain is used? Would the electroencephalograph tracings of a person speaking consciously differ from those of a glossolalist? Similarly, is there a difference between the tracings of a person talking in his sleep and a person speaking in tongues? Many persons, when speaking in their sleep, compress their language so that it closely resembles glossolalic utterances. One of the tongue-speaking women we interviewed had heard her husband talking in his sleep; she was convinced that the sounds constituted genuine glossolalia. Interestingly, the next day he began for the first time to speak in tongues.

10

Summarizing: *Is It a Spiritual Gift?*

The initial experience of glossolalia helps people to feel better. Without exception for those in the mainline Protestant churches whose experience we studied, beginning to speak in tongues was the beginning of a dramatic experience which gave the individual a sense of great joy and uplift. Depression subsided, worthlessness diminished, and a state of near-euphoria developed. Tongue-speakers were exhilarated as they validated their experience in the words of Romans 8:26: "We do not know how to pray as we ought, but the Spirit himself intercedes for us with sighs too deep for words."

A SUBJECTIVE SENSE OF WELL-BEING

One of the characteristics invariably noted by new tongue-speakers was a greater sense of power. This took the form of a stronger sense of identity and self-confidence in interpersonal relations. New tongue-speakers reported a greater sense of purpose and meaning in their lives and a deepening of its spiritual quality. Whereas religious matters often had been important to them before, after speaking in tongues they became increasingly involved with their religious convictions. They felt bolder in their business dealings, in their marriage relationships, and in _ teaching Sunday school. The conviction that they now mattered to God, to their neighbors, and to themselves resulted from the glossolalia experience.

The practitioners of glossolalia whom we surveyed were joyful and warm in one another's company. Their sense of community crossed ethnic, socioeconomic, and educational lines. Their common overwhelming experience surmounted other barriers.

We noted a tremendous openness, concern, and care for one another. We were humbled by the way in which they bore each other's burdens. They were with each other in spirit and in physical presence, and the highest ethical mandates were a part of their camaraderie. While the quality of glossolalists' lives varied in relation to their native capacities and life experiences—each had, of course, different talents for living and loving—still the evidence was impressive that their ways of dealing with life had indeed changed significantly. They reported being less annoyed by frustrations, showing greater patience in their families and a deeper love for mankind in general.

The happy effects of this phenomenon were testified to by tongue-speakers from coast to coast of the United States. The positive effects were strikingly similar from individual to individual, from group to group, and from denomination to denomination. The glossolalist noted first that there had been a maturing of his own religious life, which then expressed itself through an intense concern that one's friends and fellow church members should share the same experience. Beyond the purely spiritual dimension, the tongue-speakers felt themselves to be more effective in every area of their lives: psychological, marital, and vocational. The men and women we interviewed were uniformly candid and sincere when they talked with us about the experience of tongue-speaking and its effects.

THE CRITICISMS OF THE NONGLOSSOLALISTS

Why then have churches been so often disturbed when glossolalia is introduced into their congregations? The answer lies in the fact that glossolalists, while reporting truthfully their subjective experiences, are conscious of only one aspect of the total picture. There are many experiences in life that make one feel good, and many that make one feel closer to his fellow man, particularly when that man is a kindred spirit and a practitioner of similar kinds of behavior. However, the initiate's perspective must be supplemented by a broader view, which shows that even larger numbers are antagonized and alienated by the practice of glossolalia.

From the results of our research we conclude that although speaking in tongues is an unusual phenomenon, it is explicable in rational ways and should not cause alarm. However, because of its subjective nature it should be scrutinized by outside observers so that it can be carefully evaluated for all its positive and negative effects.

The claim is legitimate, of course, that in some ways no one can truly evaluate an experience he has not had himself. However, the claim of the outside observer has its own validity. The final judgment, we suggest, should be based on both *individual* and *community* criteria.

As behavioral scientists and as students of the religious quest, we refer to the criteria of love and creative work. The standard for evaluating any experience must be: Is it conducive to a productive life—does it help people as a whole as well as the body of men and women who comprise one's small, select company?

When measured by the building up of the wider community, glossolalia has been faulted by most outside observers. For the phenomenon has tended to have disruptive effects. Sometimes it leads to irrational excesses which result in community disintegration. For these reasons the experience has been criticized by the majority of scientific and religious groups who have studied it. We, too, must concur in this evaluation.

IS IT A SPIRITUAL GIFT?

We have shown that speaking in tongues can be learned, almost as other abilities are learned. Whether one calls the practice a gift of the Spirit is, then, a matter of individual choice. Speaking in tongues does make the individual feel better, and theologically it is perhaps possible to claim that anything that makes one feel better is in some way a gift of God. We cannot quarrel with so broad an interpretation of the meaning of "gift."

But we believe it is the *use* of glossolalia that determines whether or not it is a constructive phenomenon or rather damages and destroys. Glossolalia rarely benefits a wide segment of the community.

We hope therefore that its practioners as well as the scientists who study the phenomenon will be modest in their claims for it. For it is not uniquely spiritual; it is not uniquely the result of God's intervention in man's speech. Whether or not it is a gift of God's providential care for His people depends on varying subjective interpretations of the nature of what is spiritual and what constitutes a good gift for man.

BIBLIOGRAPHY ON GLOSSOLALIA

Books:

Abercrombie, J. *Inquiries Concerning the Intellectual Powers of Man and the Investigations of Truth.* New York: 1953.

Alighieri, Dante. *The Divine Comedy.* Henry Francis Cary, trans. New York: P. F. Collier, n.d.

American Society of Church History, *Papers.* H. M. Baird, "The Camisard Uprising, etc." Vol. II, Part I.

Anderson, Robert. *Spirit Manifestations and 'The Gift of Tongues.'* New York: Loizeaux Bros., n.d.

Andrews, Edward Deming. *The People Called Shakers.* New York: Oxford University Press, 1953.

Anquetil, L. P. *Vie du Marechal de Villars.* Vol. I. Paris: 1784.

Aquinas, Thomas. *Summa Theologica.* Great Books of the Western World. Vols. 19 and 20. Chicago: Encyclopaedia Britannica, 1952.

Bacon, Francis. *Of the Proficience and Advancement of Learning Divine and Humane.* Vol. 30. Chicago: Encyclopaedia Britannica, 1952.

Baillie, John. *The Idea of Revelation in Recent Thought.* New York: Columbia University Press, 1956.

————. *The Sense of the Presence of God.* London: Oxford University Press, 1962.

Bakan, David. *Sigmund Freud and the Jewish Mystical Tradition.* Princeton: D. Van Nostrand Co., 1958.

Baptists and the Baptism of the Holy Spirit; The Methodists and the Baptism of the Holy Spirit; Presbyterians and the Baptism of the Holy Spirit. Los Angeles: Full Gospel Business Men's Fellowship International, 1963.

Barnett, Maurice. *The Living Flame.* London: Epworth Press, 1953.

Barrett, C. K. *The Holy Spirit and the Gospel Tradition.* New York and London: Macmillan & Co., 1947.

Bartleman, Frank. *How Pentecost Came to Los Angeles.* 2nd ed., Los Angeles: Frank Bartleman, 1925.

Bauman, Louis S. *The Tongues Movement.* Winona Lake, Brethren Missionary Herald Co., 1963.

Baxter, R. *Narrative of Facts Characterizing the Supernatural Manifestations in Members of Mr. Irving's Congregation.* London: 1833.

Beadle, J. H. *Life in Utah: Mysteries and Crimes of Mormonism.* Philadelphia: National Publishing Co., 1870.

Bennett, W. J. E., ed. *The Church's Broken Unity—On Presbyterianism and Irvingism.* London: Hayes, n.d.

Benz, Ernest. *The Eastern Orthodox Church: Its Thought and Life.* Garden City, N.Y.: Doubleday Anchor Books, 1963.

Bergsma, Stuart. *Speaking with Tongues: Some Physiological and Psychological Implications of Modern Glossolalia.* Grand Rapids: Baker Book House, 1965.

Berkhof, Hendrikus. *The Doctrine of the Holy Spirit. The Annie Kinkead Warfield Lectures, 1963-64.* Richmond, Va.: John Knox Press, 1964.

Bloch-Hoell, Nils. *The Pentecostal Movement: Its Origin, Development, and Distinctive Character.* Translated from the Norwegian by the author. London: Allen & Unwin, 1964.

Boisen, Anton J. *Religion in Crisis and Custom: A Sociological and Psychological Study.* New York: Harper & Brothers, 1955.

Boyd, Frank M. *The Holy Spirit: Teacher's Manual.* Springfield, Mo.: Gospel Publishing House, n.d.

Bozzano, E. *Polyglot Mediumship.* London, 1932.

Braithwaite, W. C. *Beginnings of Quakerism.* London: Macmillan & Co., 1912.

Bray, A. E. *Revolt of the Protestants of the Cevennes.* London: Murray, 1870.

Breuer, Josef and Sigmund Freud. *Studies in Hysteria.* Boston: Beacon Press, 1958.

Brumback, Carl. *What Meaneth This? A Pentecostal Answer to a Pentecostal Question*. Springfield, Mo.: Gospel Publishing House, 1947.

———. *Suddenly . . . From Heaven: A History of the Assemblies of God*. Springfield, Mo.: Gospel Publishing House, 1961.

Büchsel, F. *Der Geist Gottes in Neuen Testament*. Gütersloh: Bertelsman, 1926.

Bulkagov, Sergius. *The Orthodox Church*. London: Centenary Press, n.d.

Burtt, Edwin A. *Types of Religious Philosophy*. New York: Harper & Row, 1951.

Butler, A. *Lives of the Saints*. 4 vols. London: 1756-59.

Caldwell, William. *Pentecostal Baptism*. Tulsa: Miracle Moments Evangelistic Association, 1963.

Calkins, M. W. *The Persistent Problems of Philosophy*. New York: Macmillan Company, 1936.

Cate, B. F. *The Nine Gifts of the Spirit Are Not in the Church Today*. Chicago: Regular Baptist Press, 1957.

Christiani, Leon. *Evidences of Satan in the Modern World*. New York: Macmillan Company, 1962.

Christenson, Laurence. *Speaking in Tongues*. Minneapolis: Bethany Fellowship, Publishers, 1968.

Clark, Elmer T. *The Small Sects in America*. Rev. ed. New York and Nashville: Abingdon Press, 1949.

Conn, Charles W. *Like a Mighty Army*. Cleveland, Tenn.: Church of God Publishing House, 1955.

———. *Pillars of Pentecost*. Cleveland, Tenn.: Pathway Press, 1956.

Conzelmann, H. *The Theology of Luke*. New York: Harper & Row, 1960.

Copleston, F. C. *Aquinas*. Baltimore: Penguin Books, 1961.

Cumont, Franz. *The Oriental Religions in Roman Paganism*. Chicago: Dover Press, 1911.

Cutten, George Barton. *Speaking with Tongues: Historically and Psychologically Considered*. New Haven: Yale University Press, 1927.

Dalton, Robert Chandler. *Tongues Like As of Fire*. Springfield, Mo.: Gospel Publishing House, 1945.

Davenport, F. M. *Primitive Traits in Religious Revivals*. London: Macmillan & Co., 1905.

Demos, Raphael. *The Philosophy of Plato*. New York: Charles Scribner's Sons, 1939.

Dermenghem, Emile. *Muhammad and the Islamic Tradition*. New York: Harper & Brothers, 1958.

Dewar, Lindsay. *The Holy Spirit and Modern Thought*. New York: Harper & Brothers, 1959.

Dodds, E. R. *The Greeks and the Irrational*. Boston: Beacon Press, 1957.

Drummond, A. *Edward Irving and His Circle: Including Some Considerations of the 'Tongues' Movement in the Light of Modern Psychology*. London: James Clark, 1937.

du Plessis, David J. *The Spirit Bade Me Go*. Dallas: David J. du Plessis, 1961.

Erikson, Erik. *Childhood and Society*. 2nd ed. New York: W. W. Norton & Co., 1963.

Ewart, Frank J. *The Phenomenon of Pentecost: A History of the Latter Rain*. St. Louis: Pentecostal Publishing House, 1947.

Felice, G. de. *History of the Protestants of France*. Barnes, trans. London: 1853.

Flournoy, Théodore. *Des Indes à la Planète Mars: Étude sur un Cas de Somnambulisme avec Glossolalie*. (From India to the Planet Mars.) Geneva: Chas. Eggimann & Co., 1900.

Foakes-Jackson, F. J., and Lake, Kirsopp. *The Beginnings of Christianity*. London: Macmillan & Co., 1933, Vol. I, p. 323 f.; Vol. I, p. 19.

Franklin, Benjamin. *Works*. J. Bigelow, ed., Vol. I.

Freemantle, Anne, ed. *A Treasury of Early Christianity*. New York: New American Library of World Literature, 1960.

Freud, Sigmund. *Collected Papers*. New York: Basic Books, 1955.

———. *Interpretation of Dreams*. New York: Basic Books, 1955.

———. *Moses and Monotheism*. New York: Vintage Books, 1955.

——— and Oscar Pfister. *Psychoanalysis and Faith: The Letters of*

Sigmund Freud and Oscar Pfister. Henrich Menz and Ernest L. Freud, eds. New York: Basic Books, 1963.

Frodsham, Stanley H. *With Signs Following: The Story of the Pentecostal Revival in the Twentieth Century.* Rev. ed. Springfield, Mo.: Gospel Publishing House, 1946 (the first edition of this book was published in 1926, also by Gospel Publishing House).

Froude, J. A. *Thomas Carlyle: A History of His Life in London.* II. New York: Harper & Brothers, 1885.

Gee, Donald. *The Pentecostal Movement.* London: Elim Publishing Co., 1941.

————. *The Pentecostal Movement, Including the Story of the War Years, 1940-47.* London: Elim Publishing Co., 1949.

————. *Concerning Spiritual Gifts.* Springfield, Mo.: Gospel Publishing House, 1947.

Görres, J. J. *La Mystique Divine, Naturelle, et Diabolique.* Trans. from the German by C. Sainte-Foi. Paris: Poussielque-Rusand, 1862.

Gould, S. B. *Virgin Saints and Martyrs.* New York: Crowell, 1923.

Grant, Carter Eldredge. *The Kingdom of God Restored.* 2nd ed. Salt Lake City: Deseret Book Co., 1955.

Gunnison, J. W. *The Mormons or Latter Day Saints in the Valley of the Great Salt Lake.* Philadelphia: J. B. Lippincott, 1860.

Hammond, W. A. *Spiritualism and Allied Causes and Conditions of Nervous Derangement.* New York: G. P. Putman, 1876.

Hartmann, Heinz. *Essays on Ego Psychology.* New York: International Universities Press, 1965.

Haskett, W. J. *Shakerism Unmasked.* Pittsfield: Walkley, 1828.

Hawthornthwaite, S. *Mr. Hawthornthwaite's Adventures Among the Mormons as an Elder During Eight Years.* Manchester, Eng., 1857.

Hayes, D. A. *The Gift of Tongues.* Cincinnati: Jennings & Graham, 1913.

Hilgard, E. *Hypnotic Susceptibility.* New York: Harcourt, Brace & World, 1965.

Hockett, Charles F., "The Problem of Universals in Language," in *Universals of Language.* Joseph H. Greenberg, ed. Cambridge, Mass.: MIT Press, 1963, pp. 1-22.

Hoekema, Anthony A. *What About Tongue-Speaking?* Grand Rapids: Wm. B. Eerdmans Publishing Co., 1966.

Horton, Harold. *The Gifts of the Spirit.* London: Assemblies of God Publishing House, 1954.

Hulme, A. J. H. and F. H. Wood. *Ancient Egypt Speaks: A Miracle of Tongues.* London: Rider, 1940.

Hutten, Kurt. *Scher, Grübler, Enthusiasten.* 6th ed. Stuttgart: Quell-Verlag, 1960.

Irving, Edward. *Collected Writings* ("Interpretation of Tongues"). Vol. V. London: Strahan, 1866.

James, William. *The Varieties of Religious Experience.* New York: Longmans, Green & Co., 1925.

Jung, C. G. *Collected Works.* New York: Pantheon Books (Bollingen Foundation), esp.:

Vol. 1, *Psychiatric Studies,* 1957.
Vol. 5, *Symbols of Transformation,* 1956.
Vol. 7, *Two Essays on Analytical Psychology,* 1953.
Vol. 9, Part I, *Archetypes and the Collective Unconscious,* 1959.
Vol. 9, Part II, *Aion,* 1959.
Vol. 11, *Psychology and Religion: West and East,* 1958.
Vol. 12, *Psychology and Alchemy,* 1953.

———. *Memories, Dreams and Reflections.* New York: Pantheon Books, 1963.

———. *Modern Man in Search of a Soul.* New York: Harcourt, Brace & Co., 1933.

———. *Psychological Types.* London: Routledge & Kegan Paul, 1953.

Jurieu, P. *Lettres Pastorales Adresses aux Fideles de France.* Rotterdam: 1686-87. English translation: 1689.

Kelsey, Morton T. *Tongue-Speaking. An Experiment in Spiritual Experience.* New York: Doubleday & Co., 1964.

Kendrick, Klaude. *The Promise Fulfilled: A History of the Modern Pentecostal Movement.* Springfield, Mo.: Gospel Publishing House, 1961.

Kennedy, J. H. *Early Days of Mormonism.* New York: Charles Scribner's Sons, 1888.

Knox, R. A. *Enthusiasm. A Chapter in the History of Religion, With Special Reference to the 17th and 18th Centuries.* New York: Oxford University Press, 1950.

Kornet, A. G. *De Pinksterbewegina en de Bijbel.* Kampen: Kok, 1963.

Krajewski, Ekkehard. *Geistesgaben. Eine Bibelarbeit über I. Korinther: 12-14.* Kassel: J. G. Oncken, 1963.

Kuyper, Abraham. *The Work of the Holy Spirit.* Henri De Vries, trans. Grand Rapids: Wm. B. Eerdmans Publishing Co., 1956.

Laffal, Julius. *Pathological and Normal Language.* New York: Atherton Press, 1965.

Lamson, D. R. *Two Years Experience Among the Shakers . . . A Condensed View of Shakerism As It Is.* Lamson: W. Boyston,

Lang, G. H. *The Earlier Years of the Modern Tongues Movement.* Wimborne, Eng.: G. H. Lang, n.d.

Lhermitte, Jacques Jean. *True and False Possession.* P. J. Hepburne-Scott, trans. New York: Hawthorne Books, 1963.

Lombard, Émile. *De la Glossolalie chez les Premiers Chrétiens et des Phénomènes Similaires.* Lausanne: Bridel, 1910.

Luchsinger, Richard and G. E. Arnold. *Voice-Speech-Language. Clinical Communicology: Its Physiology and Pathology.* Belmont, Calif.: Wadsworth Publishing Co., 1965.

McClelland, David C. "Religious Overtones in Psychoanalysis," in *The Ministry and Mental Health.* Hans Hofmann, ed. New York: Association Press, 1960, pp. 49-68.

McConkey, James H. *The Three-Fold Secret of the Holy Spirit.* Pittsburgh: Silver Publishing Society, 1897.

MacGregor, Geddes. *Introduction to Religious Philosophy.* Boston: Houghton Mifflin Co., 1959.

McIntosh, Doughlas Clyde. *The Problem of Religious Knowledge.* New York: Harper & Brothers, 1940.

McKenzie, M. *The M-H Scale. A Mental Health Scale Designed for Use with the Thematic Apperception Test.* Personal copyright, 1965.

————. *The R-F Scale. A Rigidity-Flexibility Scale Designed for Use with the Thematic Apperception Test.* Personal copyright, 1965.

Mackie, Alexander. *The Gift of Tongues.* New York: George H. Doran, 1921.

Marion, E. *La Theatre Sacre des Cevennes.* London: 1707.

Martin, Ira Jay, 3rd. *Glossolalia in the Apostolic Church. A Survey Study of Tongue-Speech.* Berea, Ky.: Berea College Press, 1960.

Mead, Frank S. *Handbook of Denominations in the United States.* 2nd rev. ed. New York and Nashville: Abingdon Press, 1961.

Metz, Donald. *Speaking in Tongues: An Analysis.* Kansas City, Mo.: Nazarene Publishing House, 1964.

Meyer, H. A. W. *Acts* ("Critical and Exegetical Commentary on the New Testament"). Edinburgh, 1873-83.

Mezer, Robert R. *Dynamic Psychiatry in Simple Terms.* New York: Springer Publishing Co., 1960.

Middleton, C. *Introductory Discourses and the Free Inquiry Into Miraculous Powers.* London, 1749.

Miller, Samuel H. *The Dilemma of Modern Belief.* New York: Harper & Row, 1963.

Molenaar, D. *De Doop Met de Heilige Geest.* Kampen: Kok, 1963.

Morris, Leon. *Spirit of the Living God.* Chicago: Inter-Varsity Press, 1960.

Mosiman, Eddison. *Das Zungenreden Geschichtlich und Psychologisch Untersucht.* Tübingen: J. C. B. Mohr, 1911.

Murphy, Gardner. *Personality: A Biosocial Approach to Origins and Structure.* New York: Harper & Brothers, 1947.

Nelson, P. C. *Bible Doctrines. A Series of Studies Based on the Statement of Fundamental Truths . . . of the Assemblies of God.* Rev. ed. Springfield, Mo.: Gospel Publishing House, 1948.

Nevis, J. L. *Demon Possession and Allied Themes.* New York: Fleming H. Revell, 1896.

Nickel, Thomas R. *The Amazing Shakarian Story.* Los Angeles: Full Gospel Business Men's Fellowship International, n.d.

Oesterreitch, T. K. *Possession.* New York: University Books, 1930.

Oliphant, Mrs. M. O. *The Life of Edward Irving.* London: Hurst & Blacketts, n.d.

Owen, John. *On the Holy Spirit.* 2 vols. Philadelphia: Protestant Episcopal Book Society, 1862.

Pearlman, Myer. *The Heavenly Gift*. Springfield, Mo.: Gospel Publishing House, 1935.

Peebles, J. M. *The Demonism of the Ages and Spirit Obsession*. Battle Creek: Peebles, 1904.

Penn-Lewis, Mrs. *The Awakening in Wales (1904-05)*. Leicester, Eng.: Overcomer Book Room, 1922.

Perkins, J. E. *The Brooding Presence and Pentecost*. Springfield, Mo.: Gospel Publishing House, 1926.

Peyrat, N. *Histoire des Pasteurs du Desert, etc.* Paris: M. Aurel Freres, 1842.

Philo. *Quis Rerum Divinarum Heres*. Loeb Classical Library. New York: G. P. Putnam, 1932.

Piaget, Jean. *The Language and Thought of the Child*. New York: Meridian Books, 1955.

Pilkington, G. *The Unknown Tongues Discovered to be English, Spanish and Latin: The Rev. Edward Irving Proved to be Erroneous in Attributing Their Utterance to the Influence of the Holy Spirit*. London: 1831.

Plato. *The Dialogues of Plato*. B. Jowett, trans. New York: Random House, 1937.

Plotinus. *The Six Enneads*. Great Books of the Western World. Vol. 17. Chicago: Encyclopaedia Britannica, 1952.

Potter, Charles Francis. *The Faiths Men Live By*. New York: Prentice-Hall Co., 1954.

Pratt, James B. *Religious Consciousness: A Psychological Study*. New York: Macmillan Company, 1921.

Pridie, J. R. *The Spiritual Gifts*. London: Robert Scott, 1921.

Rapaport, D. *Organization and Pathology of Thought*. New York: Columbia University Press, 1959.

Riggs, Ralph M. *The Spirit Himself*. Springfield, Mo.: Gospel Publishing House, 1949.

Roberts, Alexander, and Donaldson, James, eds. *The Ante-Nicene Fathers*. Grand Rapids: Wm. B. Eerdmans Co., 1950-51. (Originally published in Edinburgh, 1870-77).

Roberts, Oral. *The Baptism with the Holy Spirit and the Value of Speaking in Tongues Today*. Tulsa: Oral Roberts, 1964.

The Rudder (*Pedalion*). D. Cummings, trans. Chicago: Orthodox Christian Educational Society, 1957.

Runciman, Steven. *Byzantine Civilization*. New York: World Publishing Co., (Meridian Books), 1960.

Samarin, W. J. *Tongues of Men and Angels: the Religious Language of Pentecostalism*. New York: Macmillan Company, 1972.

Schaff, Philip. *History of the Christian Church*. New York: Charles Scribners, Sons, 1882-1910.

————. *History of the Apostolic Church*. New York: Charles Scribner's Sons, 1893.

Shaftesbury, Earl of. *Characteristics of Men, Manners, Opinions, Times*. ("Letter Concerning Enthusiasm, to my Lord Sommers.") Vol. I. London, 1737.

Sherrard, Phillip. *Athos: The Mountain of Silence*. London: Oxford University Press, 1960.

Sherrill, John L. *They Speak with Other Tongues.* London: Hodder and Stoughton Ltd., 1965.   i4.

Signs and Wonders in Rabbath-Ammon. Milwaukee: Word and Witness Publishing Co., 1934.

Simmons, J. P. *History of Tongues*. Frostproof, Fla.: n.d.

Skinner, B. F. *Verbal Behavior*. New York: Appleton-Century-Crofts, 1957.

Smiles, S. *The Huguenots in France*. London: Daldy, Isbister & Co., 1875.

Stagg, Frank E. Glenn Hinson, and Wayne E. Oates. *Glossolalia: Tongue Speaking in Biblical, Historical, and Psychological Perspective*. New York and Nashville: Abingdon Press, 1967.

Starbuck, Edwin D. *The Psychology of Religion*. New York: Charles Scribner's Sons, 1914.

Stead, W. T. *History of the Welsh Revival*. Boston: Pilgrim Press, 1905.

Steiner, Leonhard. *Mit Folgende Zeichen*. Basel: Mission für das Volle Evangelium, 1954.

Stevens, A. *The History of Methodism*. New York: Philips & Hunt, 1858.

Stiles, J. E. *The Gift of the Holy Spirit*. Burbank: Mrs. J. E. Stiles, n.d.

Stolee, H. J. *Speaking in Tongues*. Minneapolis: Augsburg Publishing House, 1963 (a reprint of *Pentecostalism,* copyrighted in 1936 by Augsburg Publishing House).

Stott, John R. W. *The Baptism and Fullness of the Holy Spirit.* Chicago: Inter-Varsity Press, 1964 (also published the same year by Inter-Varsity Fellowship, London, England).

Strack-Billerbeck. *Kommentar zum Neuen Testament aus Talmud und Mildrash.* Munich: Beck, 1926, Vol. II, p. 604.

Sullivan, Harry Stack. *The Interpersonal Theory of Psychiatry.* New York: W. W. Norton & Co., 1953.

Sundkler, Bengt G. M. *Bantu Prophets in South Africa.* 2nd ed. London: Oxford University Press, 1961.

Taber, Charles R. *French Loan Words in Sango: A Statistical Analysis of Incidence.* Hartford: Hartford Seminary Foundation (Hartford Studies in Linguistics), 1964.

Taylor, A. E. *The Faith of a Moralist.* London: Macmillan & Co., 1930.

Tennant, F. R. *Philosophical Theology.* Cambridge, Eng.: The Cambridge University Press, 1956.

Thayer, Joseph Henry. *Greek-English Lexicon of the New Testament.* New York: American Book Co., 1889.

Thomas, W. H. Griffith. *The Holy Spirit of God.* Grand Rapids: Wm. B. Eerdmans Co., 1913.

Tolkien, J. R. R. *The Lord of the Ring.* London: George Allen & Unwin, Ltd., 1954 and 1955.

Unger, Merrill F. *The Baptizing Work of the Holy Spirit.* Chicago: Scripture Press, 1953.

Van Buren, Paul M. *The Secular Meaning of the Gospel.* Paperback edition. New York: Macmillan Company, 1966.

Van Dusen, Henry P. *Spirit, Son and Father.* New York: Charles Scribner's Sons, 1958.

Vellenga, G. Y., and J. J. Kret. *Stromen van Kracht, de Nieuwe Opwekkingsbeweging.* Kampen: Kok, 1957.

von Hügel, Baron Friedrich. *The Mystical Element of Religion as Studied in Saint Catherine of Genoa and Her Friends.* London: J. J. Dent & Sons, 1927.

Walker, D. *The Gift of Tongues.* Edinburgh: T. & T. Clark, 1908.

Wilkerson, David, *The Cross and the Switchblade*. New York: (Geis) Random House, 1963.

Warfield, Benjamin B. *Miracles: Yesterday and Today. True and False*. Grand Rapids: Wm. B. Eerdmans Co., 1953 (originally published by Scribner's in 1918 under the title *Counterfeit Miracles*).

The Way of a Pilgrim. R. M. French, trans. London: S.P.C.K., 1963.

Weiss, Johannes. *The History of Primitive Christianity*. New York: Wilson-Erickson, 1937.

Weller, Rev. Philip T., trans. and ed. *The Roman Ritual*. Milwaukee: Bruce Publishing co., 1952.

Wesley, J. *Works*. Vol. V. New York: Harper, 1826-27.

White, A. D. *History of the Warfare of Science with Theology in Christiandom*. New York: Appleton, 1896.

White, Alma. *Demons and Tongues*. Bound Brook: The Pentecostal Union, 1910.

———. As above, Republished, Zarephath: Pillar of Fire, 1949.

White, Hugh. *Demonism Verified*. Ann Arbor: University Microfilms, 1963.

White, Victor. *God and the Unconscious*. New York: World Publishing Co. (Meridian Books), 1961.

Whitehead, Alfred North. *Essays in Science and Philosophy*. New York: Philosophical Library, Inc., 1948.

Whyte, Lancelot Law. *The Unconscious Before Freud*. New York: Basic Books, Inc., 1960.

Williams, Charles. *All Hallows' Eve*. London: Faber & Faber, 1945.

Wolberg, L., and Kildahl, J. *The Dynamics of Personality*. New York: Grune & Stratton, 1970.

Wood, F. H. *This Egyptian Miracle. The Restoration of Lost Speech of Ancient Egypt by Supernormal Means*. London: Rider, 1940.

Wright, A. *Some New Testament Problems*. London: Methuen, 1898.

Wright, G. Ernest. *The Rule of God*. New York: Doubleday & Co., Inc., 1960.

Zaugg, E. A. *A Genetic Study of the Spirit Phenomena in the New Testament*. Private edition, Chicago, 1917.

Zernov, Nicholas. *Eastern Christendom.* London: Weidenfeld & Nicholson, 1961.

Zodhiates, Spiros. *Speaking with Tongues,* and other titles. Six booklets. Ridgefield, N.J.: American Mission to Greeks, 1964.

Periodicals:

Abrams, M., "Baptism of the Holy Spirit at Mukti," *Missionary Review,* 19 (n.s.): 619 (August, 1906).

The Alliance Witness (May 1, 1963). Harrisburg, Pa.

America. National Catholic Weekly Review, New York, N.Y. Various issues.

American Anthropologist (February, 1956). Washington, D.C.

Bach, Marcus, "Whether There Be Tongues." *Christian Herald,* LXXXVII (May, 1964), 10-11, 20-22.

The Banner (May 31, 1963). Chicago, Ill. Various issues.

Barde, E., "La Glossolalie." *Revue de Theologie et des Questions Religieuses.* 5:125-138.

Beare, Frank W., "Speaking with Tongues: A Critical Survey of the New Testament Evidence." *Journal of Biblical Literature,* LXXXIII (September, 1964), 229-46.

Benedicite (Spring, 1963). Various issues.

Bergsma, Stuart, "Speaking with Tongues." *Torch and Trumpet.* XIV (November and December, 1964), 8-11, 9-13.

Bess, Donovan, "Speaking in Tongues: The High Church Heresy." *The Nation,* CXCVII (September 28, 1963), 173-77.

Bohon, Jean, "Les Pseudo-Glossolalies Ludiques et Magiques." *Journal Belge de Neurologie et de Psychiatrie,* Vol. 47 (April and June, 1947).

Butterfield, D. W., "Go Ye Out to Meet Him." *Voice,* XIII (December, 1965), 13-15.

The Catholic Messenger (November 7, 1963). Davenport, Iowa.

Christenson, Larry, "Speaking in Tongues . . . A Gift for the Body of Christ." Monograph, San Pedro, Calif., 1-6, n.d.

Christian Advocate (July 4, 1963). Park Ridge, Ill. Various issues.

Christian Life (July, 1963). Wheaton, Ill. Various issues.

Christianity Today (September 13, 1963). Washington, D.C.

Cincinnati *Inquirer* (January 27, 1904). Galena, Kansas.

Clemen, C., "The 'Speaking With Tongues' of the Early Christians." *Expository Times,* 10:344.

Davies, J. G., "Pentecost and Glossolalia." *Journal of Theological Studies,* III (1952), 228-31.

Dean, Robert L., "Strange Tongues. A Psychologist Studies Glossolalia." *SK&F Psychiatric Reporter,* No. 14 (May-June, 1964), 15-17.

Edman, V. Raymond, "Divine or Devilish?" *Christian Herald,* 87 (May 1964), 14-17.

Ehrenstein, Herbert Henry, "Glossolalia: First Century and Today." *The King's Business* (November, 1964), 31-34.

Eternity (July, 1963). Philadelphia, Pa.

Farrell, Frank, "Outburst of Tongues: The New Penetration." *Christianity Today,* VII (September 13, 1963), 3-7.

Finch, John G., "God-Inspired or Self-Induced?" *Christian Herald,* LXXXVII (May, 1964), 12-13, 17-19.

"Gift of Tongues in the Ancient Church," *Prospective Review,* 8:303.

Goldsmith, Henry, "The Psychological Usefulness of Glossolalia to the Believer." *View,* II (Nov. 2, 1965), 7-8.

Goodman, F., "Phonetic Analysis of Glossolalia in Four Cultural Settings." *Journal for the Scientific Study of Religion,* VIII, 227-39.

"Government Grant for Study of 'Speaking in Tongues,'" *Pastoral Psychology,* XV (September, 1964), 53-56.

Heath, R., "The Little Prophets of the Cevennes." *Contemporary Review* (January, 1886), 49:117.

Henke, F. G., "Gift of Tongues and Related Phenomena at the Present Day." *American Journal of Theology,* 13:193.

Hine, V., "Pentecostal Glossolalia: Toward a Functional Interpretation." *Journal for the Scientific Study of Religion,* VIII, 211-26.

Hitt, Russel T., "The New Pentecostalism: An Appraisal." *Eternity,* XIV (July, 1963), 10-16.

Hoffman, James W., "Speaking in tongues, 1963." *Presbyterian Life,* XVI, No. 17 (September 1, 1963), 14-17.

Hughes, Dr. Philip E., in *The Churchman* (September, 1962).

Inglis, J., "Gift of Tongues: Another View." *Theological Monthly,* 5:425.

Intercessory Missionary. Fort Wayne, Ind. Various issues.

Journal of Theological Studies (October, 1952).

Kempmeier, A., "Recent Parallels to the Miracle of Pentecost." *Open Court,* 22:492.

Kretschmer, G., "Himmelfahrt und Pfingsten." *Zeitschrift für Kirchengeschichte,* LXVI (1954-55), 209ff, esp. 223ff.

Lapsley, James N., and John H. Simpson, "Speaking in Tongues." *Princeton Seminary Bulletin,* LVIII (February, 1965), 3-18.

Le Baron, A. [pseud.], "A Case of Psychic Automatism, Including Speaking with Tongues." *Society for Psychical Research Proceedings,* XII:277.

Lindberg, D. Robert, ". . . Try the Spirits . . ." *Presbyterian Guardian,* XXXIV, No. 2 (February, 1965), 19-24.

The Living Church (July 17, 1960); January 1, 1961; March 3, May 19, June 2, and September 22, 1963).

Lohse, E., "Die Bedeutung des Pfingstberichts." *Evangelische Theologie,* XIII (1953), 422ff.

———. "Pentekoste." *Theologisches Wörterbuch zum Neuen Testament,* VI, 44-52.

Lowie, Robert H., "Dreams, Idle Dreams." *Current Anthropology,* 7:378-382 (1966), posthumous.

The Lutheran Standard (September 11, 1962).

MacDonald, William G., "Glossolalia in the New Testament." *Bulletin of the Evangelical Theological Society,* VII (Spring, 1964), 56-68 (also published in pamphlet form from the Gospel Publishing House, Springfield, Mo.).

Maeder, A. "La Langue d'un Aliene, Analyse d'un cas de Glossolalie." *Archives de Psychologie* (March, 1910).

Maglione, Paul B., "I Had Religion," *Voice,* XIII (September, 1965), 19-22.

Martin, I. J., "Glossolalia in the Apostolic Church." *Journal of Biblical Literature,* LXIII (1944), 123-30.

Martin, Sam G., "Time is Flying." *Voice*, XIII (December, 1965), 6-8.

May, L. Carlyle, "A Survey of Glossolalia and Related Phenomena in Non-Christian Religions." *American Anthropologist*, LVIII (February, 1956), 75-96.

McIntyre, John, "The Place of Imagination in Faith and Theology." *Expository Times* (October and November, 1962), Edinburgh.

Michigan Christian Advocate (April 4, 1963), Adrian, Mich.

Newbold, W. R., "Spirit Writing and 'Speaking with Tongues.'" *Popular Science Monthly*, 49:508.

Oman, John B., "On 'Speaking in Tongues': A Psychological Analysis," *Pastoral Psychology*, XIV (December, 1963), 48-51.

Pattison, E. Mansell, "Speaking in Tongues and About Tongues." *Christian Standard* (February 15, 1964), 1-2. Cincinnati, Ohio.

The Pentecost Evangel. Springfield, Mo. Various issues.

Pfister, Oskar, "Die Psychologische Enträtselung der Religiösen Glossolalie und der Automatischen Kryptographie." *Jarbuch für Psychoanalytische und Psychopathologische Forschungen*, III Bd., 1912.

Phillips, McCandlish, "And There Appeared to Them Tongues of Fire." *Saturday Evening Post* (May 16, 1964), 31-33, 39-40.

Pierson, A. T., "Speaking With Tongues," *Missionary Review*, 20: 487, 682.

Pike, James A., "Pastoral Letter Regarding 'Speaking in Tongues.'" *Pastoral Psychology*, XV (May, 1964), 56-61.

Presbyterian Life (September 1, 1963). Philadelphia, Pa.

Richet, Charles, "Xenoglossie: l'ecriture automatique en langues etrangeres." *Proceedings of the Society for Psychical Research* (1905-1907), 19:162-94 (discussion 195-266).

Runia, K., "Speaking in Tongues in the New Testament," "Speaking in Tongues Today." *Vox Reformata*, No. 4 (May, 1965), 20-29, 38-46.

———. "The Forms and Functions of Nonsense Language." *Linguistics* (1969a), 50:70-74.

———. "Glossolalia as Learned Behavior." *Canadian Journal of Theology* (1969a), 15:60-64.

Samarin, W. J. "Worship in sign language." *Acts* (Los Angeles) (1968b), 1(4).27-28.

———. "Evolution in glossolalic private language." *Anthropological Linguistics* (Bloomington, Indiana University) (1971a), 13(2). 55-67.

———. "Glossolalia as Learned Behavior." *Canadian Journal of Theology* (University of Toronto Press) (1969b). 15.60-64.

———. "The forms and functions of nonsense language." *Linguistics* (1969a), 50.70-74.

———. "The linguisticality of glossolalia." *The Hartford Quarterly* (Hartford Seminary Foundation, Hartford, Conn.) (1968a), 8(4).49-75.

———. "Glossolalia as regressive speech." *Language and Speech* (London, 1973). In press.

———. "Variation and variables in religious glossolalia." *Language in Society* (Cambridge University Press, 1972). In press.

———. "Language in resocialization." *Practical Anthropology* (Tarrytown, N.Y.) (1970), 17.269-279.

———. "What's in a word?" *Voice* (Los Angeles, October, 1971b).

Sargant, William, "Some Cultural Group Abreactive Techniques and Their Relation to Modern Treatments." *Proceedings of the Royal Society of Medicine,* Vol. 42 (May, 1949).

Schjelderup, H., "Psychologische Analyse Eines Falles von Zungenreden," *Zeitschrift für Psychologie* (1931), 122:1-27.

Schweitzer, E., "Pneuma." *Theologisches Wörterbuch zum Neuen Testament,* Vol. VI, 480 ff.

Scott, Dr. Marshal L., "Moderator's Report." *Presbyterian Life* (May, 15, 1963), n.p.

Seddon, A. E., "Edward Irving and Unknown Tongues." *Homiletic Review,* 57:103.

Shoemaker, Rev. Samuel M., *The Episcopalian* (May 15, 1963).

Shor, R., "The Frequency of Naturally Occurring 'Hypnotic-like' Experiences in the Normal College Population." *International Journal of Clinical and Experimental Hypnosis.* VIII, 151-162.

———. "Hypnosis and the Concept of the Generalized Reality-Orientation." *American Journal of Psychotherapy,* XIII, 582-602.

————. and E. Orne, "Norms on the Harvard Group Scale of Hypnotic Susceptibility, Form A." *International Journal of Clinical and Experimental Hypnosis,* XI, 39-47.

————. M. Orne and D. O'Connel, "Validation and Cross-Validation of a Scale of Self-Reported Personal Experiences Which Predict Hypnotizability." *Journal of Psychology,* LIII, 55-75.

"Symposium on Speaking in Tongues," by James H. Hanson, Gerhard Krodel, and Aarne Siirala. *dialog,* II (Spring, 1963), 152-159.

Trinity Magazine. Jean Stone, ed. Published quarterly at P. O. Box 2422, Van Nuys, Calif. Various issues.

Van Dusen, Henry Pitney, "The 'Third Force' in Christianity." *Life* (June 6, 1958), n.p.

Van Elderen, Bastiaan, "Glossolalia in the New Testament." *Bulletin of the Evangelical Theological Society,* VII (Spring, 1964), 53-58.

View. Jerry Jensen, ed. Published quarterly at 836 S. Figueroa St., Los Angeles, Calif. Various issues.

Voice. (Full Gospel Business Men's). Jerry Jensen, ed. Published monthly at 836 S. Figueroa St., Los Anegles, Calif. Various issues.

Wright, A., "Gift of Tongues: A New View." *Theological Monthly,* 5:161-272.

Zimmerman, Thomas F., "Plea for the Pentecostalists." *Christianity Today* (January 4, 1963), 11-12.

Reference:

Bibliotheca Sacra. esp. D. Green, "Gift of Tongues," 22:99.

Catholic Encyclopedia. New York: Universal Knowledge Foundation, Inc., 1907-1913.

Dictionary of the Bible. J. Hastings, ed. New York: Charles Scribner's Sons, 1909, 4:793.

Encyclopaedia Britannica. Article on "Tongues, Gift of," Vol. 22, p. 75. Chicago: Encyclopaedia Britannica, 1967.

Encyclopedia of Religion and Ethics. J. Hastings, ed. III:370. New York: Charles Scribner's Sons, 1911.

The Interpreter's Bible. New York and Nashville: Abingdon Press, 1951-55.

McClintock, J., and J. Strong. *Cyclopedia of Biblical, Theological and Ecclesiastical Literature.* 10:479. New York: 1869-81.

Nicene and Post-Nicene Fathers. First Series: Philip Schaff, ed. Second Series: Philip Schaff and Henry Wace, eds. Grand Rapids: Wm. B. Eerdmans Co., 1952 and 1956.

Schaff-Herzog Encyclopedia of Religious Knowledge. P. Feine, "Speaking with Tongues," XI:37. Grand Rapids: Baker, 1960.

Yearbook of American Churches. 31st annual edition. Benson Y. Landis, ed. New York: Office of Publication and Distribution, National Council of the Churches of Christ in the U.S.A., 1963.

Unpublished Material:

Forge, James Norman. *The Doctrine of Miracles in the Apostolic Church.* Unpublished Master's Dissertation, Dallas Theological Seminary, 1951.

Lester, Arthur D. Glossolalia: *A Psychological Evaluation.* Unpublished seminar paper, Southern Baptist Theological Seminary, Louisville, Ky., 1965.

Lovekin, Arthur Adams. *Glossolalia: A Critical Study of Alleged Origins, the New Testament and the Early Church.* Unpublished Master's Thesis, Graduate School of Theology, University of the South, Sewanee, Tenn., 1962.

Nida, Eugene A. *Glossolalia: A Case of Pseudo-Linguistic Structure.* Unpublished paper delivered at the 39th Annual Meeting of the Linguistic Society of America (New York City, December 28, 1964).

Oates, Wayne E. *Ecstaticism.* Unpublished paper, Duke University, 1943.

Preliminary Report. Unpublished study by the Division of Pastoral Services of the Episcopal Diocese of California, Study Commission on Glossolalia, 1963. Copies can be obtained from the Diocesan Headquarters at 1055 Taylor St., San Francisco, Calif.

Read, Allen Walker. *Dreamed Words: Their Implications for Linguistic Theory.* Unpublished manuscript, 12 pp., 1967.

Samarin, W. J. *Glossolalia as regressive speech.* Paper given at the Summer Meeting of the Linguistic Society of America, Columbus, Ohio, 1970a.

————. *The Glossolalist's "Grammar of Use."* Paper given at the Annual Meeting of the American Anthropological Association, San Diego, Calif., 1970b.

————. *Evolution in Glossolalic Private Language.* Ms.

————. *Worship in Sign Language.* Acts (Los Angeles, Calif.) Vol. 1, No. 4, 27-28 (1968b).

————. "Theory of order with disorderly data." Paper read at the Annual Meeting of the American Anthropological Association, New York City (November, 1971).

————. "The language of religion." Paper read at the Annual Meeting of the Society for the Scientific Study of Religion, Chicago (October, 1971).

Shumway, C. W. *A Critical History of Glossolalia.* Unpublished Dissertation. Boston University, Boston, 1919.

Vivier, L. M. Van Eetveldt. *Glossolalia.* Unpublished Dissertation for the University of Witwatersand, Johannesburg, South Africa, 1960.

Wolfram, Walter A. *The Sociolinguistics of Glossolalia.* Unpublished M. A. Thesis. Hartford Seminary Foundation, Hartford, Conn., 1966, 115 pp.

The most commonly cited scriptural references to glossolalia are from *Isaiah, Joel,* the four Gospels (*Matthew, Mark, Luke,* and *John*), the *Psalms* (e.g., 51:10, 11; 63:3, 5; 139:1, 5, 7; 150), the *Acts* (numerous references), and the Pauline corpus (chiefly *Corinthians*).

Index

abuses of gifts of tongues, 9-10
Acts of the Apostles, 13
American Lutheran Church, the,
ix-x
anger, 68-71
anxiety crisis, 57-59
Augustine of Hippo, 15
authority figure
  falling out with, 79
  glossolalists dependent in presence
  of, 41-43
  relationships of glossolalists to, 50,
  65, 80-81
autosuggestion, glossolalia as form of,
28

Bennett, Dennis F., 20, 34
Bertrand, Louis, 16
Blessed Trinity Society, 22
Bredesen, Harold, 33

charismatic gifts, 10
Christenson, Laurence, 23-24
Chrysostom, 15
church, the
  and tongue-speakers, 70-71
  and tongue-speaking, 8-9, 85

collective unconscious, Jung's theory
  of, 27, 29, 30
community
  glossolalists' sense of, 84
  wider, the, 85, 86
congregations and glossolalia, 66-68,
  85
I Corinthians 12:10, 11, 13
  14:21, 12
  14:22, 13
criteria of love and creative work, 85
Cutten, George Barton, 24-26

deautomatization, 61
dependent transference, 50
depression, feelings of, 45-47, 63, 83
du Plessis, David, 20-21, 53

Edman, V. Raymond, 26
ego control, 36-37
ego, the, 36
emotional maturity and use of glossolalia, 59-60
euphoria, feelings of, 51-53, 64, 65,
  83
  transference relationship brings,
  79-80

107